Writing for Dollars,
Writing to Please

Writing for Dollars, Writing to Please

The Case for Plain Language in Business, Government, and Law

Joseph Kimble

*For Jim Thelen —
A prize-winner and friend.
Joe Kimble
June 2017*

CAROLINA ACADEMIC PRESS

Durham, North Carolina

Library of Congress Cataloging-in-Publication Data

Kimble, Joseph.
  Writing for dollars, writing to please: the case for plain
  language in business, government, and law / Joseph Kimble.
        p. cm.
  Includes bibliographical references and index.
  ISBN: 978-1-61163-191-3 (alk. paper)
  1. Law—United States—Language. 2. Law—United States—
  Terminology. 3. Legal composition. 4. Government report
  writing—United States. I. Title.

KF250.K535 2012
340'.14—dc23   2012013645

Carolina Academic Press
700 Kent Street
Durham, North Carolina 27701
Telephone (919) 489-7486
Fax (919) 493-5668
www.cap-press.com

Printed in the United States of America

For two boys named Axel and Jet Pierce —
and their G-Ma MaryAnn

Contents

Preface xiii

Part One: A Personal Story   **1**

Part Two: The Elements of Plain Language   **5**

**Part Three: Answering the Critics
(by Dispelling the Myths)**   **11**

1. Plain language is not anti-literary, anti-
   intellectual, unsophisticated, drab, ugly, bland,
   babyish, or base 11

2. The idea of plain language is not too vague to
   be useful 14

3. Plain language is not "text-based" rather than
   "reader-based"; it has always been concerned with
   whether the text works for readers and has long
   advocated testing on readers 16

4. Plain language involves much more than just
   simple words and short sentences 20

5. Regardless of what readers may expect in legal
   and official documents, they certainly prefer
   plain language 23

6. There is time to write in plain language — or at
   least to make a serious start...................................... 25

7. The push for plain language will not result in less
   work and less prestige for lawyers; it could even
   produce more work, and it will surely improve
   their image 28

8. Proponents do not imagine that plain language
   will be intelligible to everyone; they do expect
   writers to make documents intelligible to the
   greatest possible number of intended readers 31

9. Plain language is not subverted by the need to use technical terms 35

10. Plain language is not imprecise; in fact, it's more precise than traditional legal and official style 37

Part Four: Some Historical Highlights   45

Publications

1. U.S.: David Mellinkoff's Book *The Language of the Law* 47

2. U.S.: Richard Wydick's Book *Plain English for Lawyers* 47

3. U.S.: "Plain Language" Column in the *Michigan Bar Journal* 48

4. U.S.: Rudolf Flesch's Works and Readability Formulas 49

5. UK: Ernest Gowers's Book *The Complete Plain Words* 51

6. UK: Renton Committee Report on Legislation 52

7. Australia: Michèle Asprey's Book *Plain Language for Lawyers* 53

Laws and Rules

8. U.S.: New York's Plain-English Law — and Other State Statutes That Followed 54

9. U.S.: Securities and Exchange Commission's Plain-English Rules and *Plain English Handbook* 56

10. U.S.: Plain Writing Act of 2010 57

11. European Union: Unfair Contract Terms Directive 59

12. South Africa: Constitution 60

13. South Africa: Consumer Protection Act 62

Projects and Activities

14. U.S.: Citibank's Loan Note 64

15. U.S.: Redrafting of Federal Court Rules 64

16. Canada: Reports on Access to the Law and
    Events That Followed 66

17. Canada: Training in Provincial Securities
    Commissions and the Rewriting of
    Investment-Industry Rules 68

18. UK: Government-Wide Review of Forms 69

19. UK: Tax-Law Revision 70

20. Norway: Civil-Service Project 71

21. Australia: NRMA's Car-Insurance Policy 72

22. Australia: Progress in Major Law Firms 73

23. Australia: Format of Legislation 75

24. New Zealand: WriteMark and Plain
    English Power 76

Organizations

25. U.S.: Document Design Center at the
    American Institutes for Research 78

26. U.S.: Federal-Employee PLAIN Group and
    the Clinton–Gore Initiatives 80

27. U.S.: Center for Plain Language 81

28. Canada: Plain Language Association
    International 82

29. Canada: Canadian Legal Information Centre
    and Its Plain Language Centre 83

30. Canada: Alberta Law Reform Institute 85

31. Canada: Plain Language Service at the
    Canadian Public Health Association 86

32. UK: Clarity — The International Association
    Promoting Plain Legal Language 87

33. UK: Plain English Campaign and Plain
    Language Commission 88

34. European Union: Fight the Fog and the Clear
    Writing Campaign 91

35. Nordic Countries: Language Councils 92
36. Sweden: Division for Legal and Linguistic
    Draft Revision, and the Plain Swedish Group 96
37. Australia: Law Reform Commission of Victoria 97
38. Australia: Centre for Plain Legal Language 99
39. New Zealand: Law Commission and the
    Parliamentary Counsel Office 100
40. Commonwealth Countries: Commonwealth
    Association of Legislative Counsel 101

Part Five: The Extraordinary Benefits 103

Saving Time and Money

1. U.S.: Federal Communications Commission —
   Regulations 107
2. U.S.: Veterans Benefits Administration —
   Form Letters 108
3. U.S.: Veterans Benefits Administration —
   Form Letters 111
4. U.S.: Naval Officers — Business Memos 112
5. U.S.: State of Washington — Consumer
   Documents 113
6. U.S.: Arizona Department of Revenue —
   Form Letters 116
7. U.S.: Los Angeles County — Consumer
   Documents and Phone Messages 117
8. Canada: Alberta Agriculture, Food, and Rural
   Development — Forms 118
9. UK: British Government — Forms 119
10. UK: Royal Mail — Form 121
11. Sweden: Agency for Higher Education Services—
    Online Forms and E-Mail 121
12. New Zealand: Ministry of Internal Affairs —
    Form 123

13. Australia: Victorian Government — Legal Form 124

14. Australia: Family Court of Australia — Divorce Forms 124

15. U.S.: Cleveland Clinic — Billing Statements 125

16. U.S.: Allen-Bradley Company — Computer Manuals 125

17. U.S.: General Electric Company — Software Manuals 127

18. U.S.: Sabre Travel Information Company — Software Booklet 127

19. U.S.: Federal Express — Operations Manuals 128

20. U.S.: Key Bank — Call-Center Manual 129

21. Canada: Banking Industry — Communications Among Employees 129

22. U.S.: Homebuyers — Good-Faith Estimates 130

23. U.S.: General Public — Payday Loans 132

Pleasing and Persuading Readers

24. U.S.: Judges and Lawyers — Various Legal Passages 135

25. U.S.: Appellate Judges and Law Clerks — Appellate Briefs 137

26. U.S.: Lawyers — Judicial Opinions 139

27. U.S.: Judges — Lawsuit Papers 141

28. U.S.: General Public — Various Legal Passages 143

29. U.S.: General Public — Government Regulations 144

30. U.S.: General Public — Statute 145

31. U.S.: General Public — Jury Instructions 145

32. U.S.: General Public — Jury Instructions 146

33. U.S.: General Public — Jury Instructions 148

34. U.S.: General Public — Court Forms 148

35. U.S.: General Public — Class-Action Notices 149

36. U.S.: Law Students and State-Agency
    Employees — Contract 151

37. South Africa: Lawyers and the General
    Public — Various Legal Documents 153

38. Australia: Lawyers — Legislation 154

39. U.S.: General Public — Tax Forms 154

40. U.S.: General Public — Ballot Instructions 155

41. U.S.: Naval Officers — Business Memos 157

42. U.S.: Army Officers — Business Memos 158

43. Australia: Insurance Companies — Office
    Manual 159

44. U.S.: General Public — Medical-Consent
    Forms 159

45. U.S.: General Public — Medical Pamphlet 160

46. U.S.: General Public — Medication Warning
    Labels 161

47. Canada: General Public — Patient-
    Information Booklet 162

48. U.S.: Investors — 10-K Filings 163

49. U.S.: Investors — Annual Reports 165

50. UK: Institution of Chemical Engineers —
    Technical Literature 166

PREFACE

These pages round out a large part of a life's work — as a teacher, speaker, and writer — campaigning for plain legal language. As noted in part 1, I've concentrated over the years on the writing guidelines that provide a route to clarity and simplicity, the false criticisms that stand in the way, and the mounting evidence that plain language pays off — considerably — in the end. In a sense, this book is a second edition of previous writings on those subjects. The title itself is the title of an article in volume 6 of *The Scribes Journal of Legal Writing*, and the title of part 3 comes from an article in volume 5 of the *Journal*. Parts of those two articles, and other articles as well, are incorporated in this second edition.

But the book is still new. I've reworked, rearranged, and updated much of the previous material. I've also added to it. Part 3 expands on the myths and realities. Part 4 is entirely new (and was quite an undertaking). Part 5 doubles the number of empirical studies that I reported on in earlier articles. In any case, I hope readers will like having this information all in one place.

Now, a few miscellaneous points:

- There is no index. This is not a book in which you'll be looking up topics and names. The detailed table of contents, the extensive headings and subheadings, and the occasional introductory notes should provide plenty of orientation.
- The references generally follow legal-citation form. Thus, in "64 Clarity 5," for example, the first number is the volume, and the second is the page. The abbreviation "J." stands for "Journal," "B.J." is "Bar Journal," and "L. Rev." is "Law Review." Other abbreviations in periodicals should be fairly obvious,

even to nonlegal readers. I did spell out some words
that I thought might not be.

- Internet citations, URLs, are always a challenge.
Besides being ugly, they come and go. But they were
all last accessed in March 2012, and I printed off copies of all the shorter ones.

- Perhaps the two journals cited most often are *Clarity* and the *Michigan Bar Journal* (which publishes
the "Plain Language" column). You can find most of
those articles by running a Google search for "Clarity International" or "Plain Language Column." I've
also added "available at" URLs to many of the citations, especially when it might not be obvious where
to find an electronic version if there is one.

- I have copies of everything cited in the footnotes. If
you need an item and can't get it, I'll try to send it to
you on request (unless it's a book).

- As a small concession to international preferences, I
used periods with "U.S." but not "UK" or "EU."

- The book is not flooded with before-and-after examples. Short ones appear in appropriate places, and
you can find longer ones to your heart's content
through the references — like those on page 5, note
1. There's little justification these days for profess-
ing ignorance about what plain language looks like
or for claiming that it can't be done.

～

Four Thomas Cooley Law School graduates — Robert
Webb, Kelly Stewart, Thomas Myers, and Rachel
Glogowski — each spent loads of time helping with different aspects of this book. Their work was superb, and I'm
heavily in their debt.

I owe others as well. Three readers — Annetta Cheek,
Martin Cutts, and David Schultz — reviewed the entire

manuscript and had valuable comments on page after page. Others read and greatly improved parts of the book: Joseph Spaniol, Robert Eagleson, Michèle Asprey, Ginny Redish, Karen Schriver, and Mark Cooney. Matthew Butterick offered many suggestions that sharpened the typography. And Karen Magnuson did her usual peerless job of copyediting. To all these friends and colleagues, my heartfelt thank-you for your contributions.

Finally, a word of thanks to Cindy Hurst, my assistant for more than 25 years. She keeps the work on track — with greater equanimity than I deserve.

PART ONE

A Personal Story

Flash back to the late '60s. I entered law school and started reading law. It impressed me as new and different, challenging, complex, somewhat mysterious, elevated but by and large not very literary, far more dull than lively, sprung from real-life episodes that became dry in the legal dissection, a chore to undertake. Thus, myriad passages like the one below from the Hairy-Hand Case, made famous in the movie *The Paper Chase*. (What produced the hairy hand? A surgeon had grafted skin from the patient's chest onto his scarred hand.)

> It is unnecessary to determine at this time whether the argument of the defendant, based upon "common knowledge of the uncertainty which attends all surgical operations," and the improbability that a surgeon would ever contract to make a damaged part of the human body "one hundred per cent perfect" would, in the absence of countervailing considerations, be regarded as conclusive, for there were other factors in the present case which tended to support the contention of the plaintiff.[1]

In other words:

> The doctor argues that everybody knows surgery is uncertain and no surgeon would ever promise a "perfect" result. Those arguments might be conclusive

---

[1] *Hawkins v. McGee*, 146 A. 641, 643 (N.H. 1929).

if they stood alone. But the patient produced other evidence that supported his interpretation of the doctor's words.

For three years, I never questioned the legal style. That's the way it was and had to be. Law was a sophisticated, rigorous, highly intellectual discipline that needed a writing style to match. Doesn't every advanced field and profession? (And besides, I imagined that some undergraduates at the University of Michigan just might be semi-impressed by a guy's sounding like an aspiring lawyer. One of them observed that I "talked a lot about the Tigers [baseball team] and torts.")

How could I have been so accepting, so divorced from what I had studied and done? Went to a good private high school, Cranbrook, as a boarding student (a small-town kid on a scholarship, feeling like a fish out of water). Had to memorize literary pieces and recite them in class. ("If it were done when 'tis done . . . ." "Shall I compare thee to a summer's day?") Won a few writing awards in a competition sponsored by the *Detroit News*. Studied English at Amherst College: all of Shakespeare, all of English poetry going back to Chaucer, the great English novels, even a course in Dostoyevsky. Wrote paper after paper, and a senior thesis on Thomas Hardy. Graduated with honors. You might have thought I would have approached legal style with a sharper critical faculty. But it never occurred to me that anything was wrong. Maybe I was too distracted by the diversions of Ann Arbor — and of the times.

Of course, as I remember, none of the professors ever criticized the writing in an opinion or a rule either. Never a suggestion that something wasn't well written or was unnecessarily complicated. And this was before any law school had a serious legal-writing program to counter the daily diet of legalese. So no — it didn't hit me until later.

Now jump forward to the mid-'70s. I was working on the staff of the Michigan Supreme Court, after a couple of years writing research memos for the Michigan Court of

Appeals. The Supreme Court was responsible for all the Michigan court rules — a responsibility that often meant drafting new or amended ones. This was not considered glamorous work, so it fell to me. Like every other lawyer of my generation — and the great majority of lawyers practicing today — I had no training in how to draft. None. So I wandered downstairs to the state law library and discovered just about the only current book on the subject, the first edition of Reed Dickerson's *Fundamentals of Legal Drafting.* I began to browse through it and noticed several pages listing words and phrases. They were listed on the left side under the heading "Instead of." Then on the right side was the plainer, simpler equivalent of each one. And it finally started to dawn on me. Why *do* we say *pursuant to* instead of *under*? Why do we say *prior to* instead of *before*? Why do we say *approximately* instead of *about*, and *frequently* instead of *often*? It didn't take long for me to become a convert to plain language.

I made one other discovery at about the same time, while in a variety store (of all places) during a lunch hour: I spotted a cheap paperback edition of a book called *Modern American Usage*, written by Wilson Follett and completed by Jacques Barzun after Follett's death. I had used writing handbooks before, but this one was different — eloquent and forceful, sharply discriminating, devoted entirely to matters of usage and style, and passionately on the side of simplicity. I had stumbled into the world of books on language and style, and Barzun became an early inspiration.

That was 35 years ago. The awakening began with vocabulary, but I have learned along the way that clear writing involves much more than the choice of words. I've tried to put together and illustrate the main techniques for writing in plain language. I've tried endlessly to debunk the myths and misconceptions about plain language. I've tried to collect and summarize the empirical evidence for the benefits of plain language. This book reflects all those efforts.

The journey that started with Dickerson and Barzun has benefited from too many teachers to name, except maybe in a prominent footnote that comes with deep gratitude.[2] The journey probably culminated in my work redrafting the Federal Rules of Civil Procedure and Federal Rules of Evidence. I'm afraid that if some fortune-teller had told my civil-procedure and evidence profs at Michigan that I'd someday do that work, they would have gasped. Me too.

---

[2] Richard Wydick, Barbara Child, Bryan Garner, Ginny Redish, Joseph Williams, David Elliott, Mark Adler, Martin Cutts, Robert Eagleson, Christopher Balmford, Peter Butt, Michèle Asprey.

PART TWO

The Elements of Plain Language

This is the fourth version of these guidelines. They were originally meant for printed legal documents, but I have tinkered and tweaked, and now they should work more universally. Of course, bare guidelines are not enough: they need to be explained and illustrated, and applied with an eye for possible exceptions and occasional tension between them. For that depth of understanding, writers need to consult the plain-language literature.[1]

A. In General

1. As the starting point and at every point, design and write the document in a way that best serves the readers. Your main goal is to convey your ideas with the greatest possible clarity.

2. Resist the urge to sound formal. Relax and be natural (but not too informal). Try for the same unaffected tone you would use if you were speaking to the reader in person.

---

[1] *See* Joseph Kimble, *Lifting the Fog of Legalese: Essays on Plain Language* appendix 2 (Carolina Academic Press 2006) (containing a select "bookshelf").

3. Omit unnecessary detail. Boil down the information to what your reader needs to know.

4. Use examples as needed to help explain the text.

5. Whenever possible, test consumer documents on a group of typical users — and improve the documents as need be.

B. Design

1. Take pains to make the document look inviting and easy to read.

2. Create a table of contents for long documents.

3. Use 10- to 12-point type for body text on paper, at least 12 point online, and a legible font. Among the good ones for paper: Book Antiqua, Century Schoolbook, Garamond, Goudy Old Style, Palatino. And for the screen: Georgia, Gill Sans, Verdana. But different fonts at the same point size may look large or small, so try different sizes.

4. Try to use between 45 and 70 characters a line.

5. Use ample white space in margins (more than an inch on standard paper) and between lines (about 25% of the point size). Put more space above headings than below. Add extra space above and below a vertical list, and a little extra between the items.

6. Put most headings and subheadings flush left, use boldface, try for no more than two levels, and distinguish between the levels (typically through font size). Limit centered headings to short ones at the highest level of breakdown.

7. Avoid using all-capital letters and underlining. And avoid overusing initial capitals for common nouns (*this agreement, trust, common stock* — in lowercase).

8. Consider using diagrams, tables, and charts in place of continuous text, or at least as an aid to understanding it.

9. In consumer documents, make liberal use of bulleted lists. Try them in legal documents as well. And in any vertical list, bulleted or numbered, use hanging indents: don't let a later line come back farther than the first word in the first line.

C. Organization

1. Try to begin the document and the main divisions with one or two paragraphs that introduce and summarize what follows. In legal briefs and memos, include your answer in the summary.

2. Use short sections, or subdivide longer ones.

3. Show the structure with headings and subheadings, and make them informative. ("How to Apply for a Grant." Not: "Applications.") In consumer documents, try putting at least the main headings in the form of questions that the reader might ask.

4. Put related material together.

5. Order the parts in a logical sequence. Normally, put the more important before the less important, the general before the specific, and the ordinary before the extraordinary. For instructions or a process, use chronological order.

6. Break up long paragraphs. Keep most of them under six sentences (or 100 words) on paper and under four sentences (or 60 words) online.

7. Make sure in each paragraph that the topic sentence not only summarizes the main idea but also connects it logically to the previous paragraph.

8. Use transitions (*But*, *So*, *Another purpose*) as needed to link your ideas and introduce new ones.

9. Minimize cross-references. Be extremely stingy with global cross-references (*except as otherwise provided herein*).

10. Minimize definitions. If you have more than a few, put them in a separate section at the end of the document.

D. Sentences

1. Prefer short and medium-length sentences. As a guideline, keep the average length to about 20 words.

2. Don't pile up a series of items — conditions, consequences, rules — before the main clause. If the items are at all complicated, put them in a vertical list at the end of the sentence.

3. In most sentences, put the subject near the beginning; keep it short and concrete; make it something the reader already knows about (old information); and make it the agent of the action in the verb.

4. Put the central action in strong verbs, not in abstract nouns. ("If the seller delivers the goods late, the buyer may cancel the contract." Not: "Late delivery of the goods is grounds for cancellation of the contract.") Uncover hidden verbs.

5. Keep the subject near the verb, and the verb near the object (or complement). Avoid intrusive phrases and clauses.

6. Put the strongest point in the sentence, your most important information, at the end — where the emphasis falls.

7. Prefer the active voice. But use the passive voice if the agent is unknown or unimportant. Or use it if, for continuity, you want to focus attention on the object of the action instead of the agent. ("No more legalese. It has been ridiculed long enough.")

8. Connect modifying words to what they modify. Be especially careful with a series: make clear whether the modifier applies to one or more than one item. (Examples of ambiguity: "educational institutions or corporations"; "a felony or misdemeanor involving dishonesty.")

E. Words

1. Prefer familiar words — usually the shorter ones — that are simple and direct and human.

2. Avoid unnecessary jargon, especially hardcore legalese: *here-*, *there-*, and *where-* words (*hereby, therein, wherefore*); doublets and triplets (*any and all*; *give, devise, and bequeath*); needless Latin (*arguendo, inter alia, silentio*); and all the rest (*and/or, provided that, pursuant to, the instant case*).

3. Explain technical terms that your readers might not understand.

4. Omit unnecessary words. For one thing, keep prepositional phrases in check. Treat the word *of* as a good indicator of possible flab (*the duty of the landlord, an order of the court*).

5. Replace wordy phrases. Take special aim at multiword prepositions (*prior to, with regard to, in connection with*).

6. Avoid multiple negatives.

7. Banish *shall*; use *must* instead.

8. In consumer documents, consider making the consumer "you" and the organization "we."

9. Think twice about creating or using an initialism that will be new to your readers (*Committee on Plain Language (CPL)*).

10. Be consistent; use the same term for the same thing, especially in legal drafting.

PART THREE

Answering the Critics
(by Dispelling the Myths)

In the mind of anyone who cares to review the evidence and literature, the myths about plain language should have long since been obliterated. For at least 50 years, one expert after another has debunked them.[1] But they are stubborn and pernicious. They keep spooking us, dissuading us, fooling us, and providing us with an excuse for clinging to legalese and officialese. So let's try again to put them to rest. No need for stakes through the heart. These are mere apparitions, chimeras, hobgoblins. Know the truth, and fear not.

1. Plain language is not anti-literary, anti-intellectual, unsophisticated, drab, ugly, bland, babyish, or base.

This charge of debasing the language is loaded with irony. If anything is anti-literary, drab, and ugly, it's traditional legal

---

[1] *See, e.g.*, Michèle M. Asprey, *Plain Language for Lawyers* 12–15 (4th ed., Fed'n Press 2010); Law Reform Comm'n of Victoria, *Plain English and the Law* 45–62 (1987; repr. 1990); David Mellinkoff, *The Language of the Law* 285–454 (Little, Brown & Co. 1963); Robert W. Benson, *The End of Legalese: The Game Is Over*, 13 N.Y.U. Rev. L. & Social Change 519, 558–67 (1984–1985); Wayne Schiess, *What Plain English Really Is*, 9 Scribes J. Legal Writing 43, 51–71 (2003–2004).

and official writing — those bastions of inflation and obscurity.

Take legal writing, which has been ridiculed and criticized for centuries.[2] David Mellinkoff describes it as wordy, unclear, pompous, and dull.[3] John Lindsey says that law books are "the largest body of poorly written literature ever created by the human race."[4] Bryan Garner agrees: "[W]e [lawyers] have a history of wretched writing, a history that reinforces itself every time we open the law books."[5]

The heritage of plain English is just the opposite. As Garner explains: "It is the language of the King James Version of the Bible, and it has a long literary tradition in the so-called Attic style of writing."[6] Plain English is the style of Abraham Lincoln, and Walt Whitman, and Mark Twain, and Justice Holmes, and George Orwell, and Winston Churchill, and E.B. White. Plain words are eternally fresh and fit. More than that, they are capable of great power and dignity: "And God said, Let there be light: and there was light. And God saw the light, that it was good."[7] Or Shakespeare: "[A]nd, when he shall die/Take him and cut him out in little stars/ And he will make the face of heaven so fine/That all the world will be in love with night/And pay no worship to the garish sun."[8] Or Thoreau: "If you have built castles in the air, your

---

2   *See* Joseph Kimble, *Lifting the Fog of Legalese: Essays on Plain Language* appendix 1 (Carolina Academic Press 2006) (quoting a "litany of complaints" going back to King Edward VI in the 16th century).

3   Mellinkoff, *supra* n. 1, at 24.

4   John M. Lindsey, *The Legal Writing Malady: Causes and Cures*, N.Y. L.J., Dec. 12, 1990, at 2.

5   Bryan A. Garner, *The Elements of Legal Style* 2 (2d ed., Oxford U. Press 2002).

6   Bryan A. Garner, *Garner's Dictionary of Legal Usage* 680 (3d ed., Oxford U. Press 2011).

7   *Genesis* 1:3–4.

8   *Romeo and Juliet* act 3, scene 2.

work need not be lost; that is where they should be. Now put the foundations under them."[9]

Why would we ever think that a profusion of fancy-sounding words in any way equates with wit, wisdom, depth, vitality, importance, usefulness, or reliability? How can we be so blind or indifferent to the manifold failings of legal and official style — in all their clotted, confounding verbosity?

It's true that the term *plain language* is open to at least three misinterpretations. It may suggest something that's colorless, that concentrates only on vocabulary, and that's facile.

But it need not be colorless; it can be lively and expressive in the right context, such as a persuasive legal brief. And in every context, plain language can be elegant in its clarity and simplicity. After all, most legal and official documents are not read for pleasure: nobody expects rhetorical flourishes or stylistic flair in a contract; nobody curls up with a Medicare brochure. Readers just want to get the message, without travail.

Nor does modern-day plain language center on vocabulary, as I discuss under myth 4 below. It embraces all the many techniques for clear communication.

As for achieving it, that's never easy. Anyone can complicate matters; it's much harder to simplify without oversimplifying, and only the best minds and best writers can hit that mark. In fact, writing simply and directly only *looks* easy. It takes skill and sweat and fair time to do the job. Or in Jacques Barzun's memorable line: "Simple English is no one's mother tongue. It has to be worked for."[10]

We are too far down the road to swap the term *plain language* for something else. A strong, extensive body of supporting literature has developed around it. More than any other term, such as *clear communication*, it signifies a new

---

[9] Henry David Thoreau, *Walden Pond* chapter 18.

[10] Jacques Barzun, *Teacher in America* 48 (Little, Brown & Co. 1945).

attitude and a fundamental change from past practices. It strikes a chord with the public. And once again, it can claim a glorious literary heritage.

2. The idea of plain language is not too vague to be useful.

Much confusion attends the popular debating point that an idea or term is vague and needs to be defined. At some point, all natural language is vague: you can imagine facts at the margins of application, facts that the term might or might not reach. Does *highway* include the median? The shoulder? The stop sign? In another place, I listed 16 obviously vague terms (and could have added many more) in just the first six rules of the Federal Rules of Criminal Procedure.[11]

Thus, it's no criticism of plain language that it cannot be precisely, mathematically defined; neither can most terms, legal or otherwise. The question is whether we can arrive at the right degree of vagueness — one that makes the term suitably clear and at the same time avoids drilling down for more and more detail in the illusory quest for perfect precision. The answer is yes: the meaning of *plain language* can be made clear — and in different ways.

Over the years, a great many definitions have been put forward. In 1992, I surveyed a number of them.[12] Some are very general and look mainly to the text. The original plain-English law, in New York, requires simply that a consumer contract be "(1) Written in a clear and coherent manner using words with common and everyday meanings; (2) Appropriately divided and captioned by its various

---

[11] *How to Mangle Court Rules and Jury Instructions*, in *Lifting the Fog of Legalese*, *supra* n. 2, at 105, 120.

[12] *Plain English: A Charter for Clear Writing*, 9 Thomas M. Cooley L. Rev. 1, 11–16 (1992).

sections."[13] Other definitions are very general and look mainly to the readers. Here's one from the U.S. Center for Plain Language: information is in plain language if the intended audience can "quickly and easily find what they need, understand what they find, and act appropriately on that understanding."[14] Some definitions are stated as guidelines like those in part 2 of this book: a document is — or is more likely to be — in plain language if it follows a set of guidelines or criteria. Of course, the guidelines may vary in number and specificity (e.g., "use a readable type size" versus "use 10- to 12-point type for text"). Yet they are, for the most part, remarkably consistent. Finally, some advocates would equate *plain language* with meeting one of several readability formulas, the best known of which are associated with Rudolf Flesch: the Flesch Reading-Ease Score and the Flesch–Kincaid Grade Level.

The most comprehensive treatment of definitions appears in *Clarity* No. 64, in an article written by Annetta Cheek.[15] Cheek's article identifies no fewer than 25 definitions — and acknowledges that there are many more. It groups the definitions into three of the categories just mentioned:

- Those based on numbers or formulas (such as the Flesch tests).
- Those focused on elements or guidelines (such as those in this book).
- Those focused on outcomes with readers (such as the find & understand & use definition from the Center for Plain Language).

---

[13] N.Y. Gen. Oblig. Law § 5-702(a).

[14] http://centerforplainlanguage.org/about-plain-language.

[15] Annetta Cheek, *Defining Plain Language*, 64 Clarity 5 (Nov. 2010); for more about *Clarity* No. 64, see part 4 of this book, highlight 28.

The article reviews the strengths and weaknesses of each category of definition. And it acknowledges the need for flexibility, depending on the document's purpose and the readers' ability.

Ultimately, the article recommends a definition like the following, which is in the third category:

> A communication is in plain language if its wording, structure, and design are so clear that the intended readers can easily find what they need, understand it, and use it.[16]

At the same time, though, the article emphasizes that guidelines are needed for getting us to this result and that readability measures can help us gauge whether we did well — or, more accurately, whether we probably fell short. All three categories of definitions play a part.

So you can pick your definition, and it can be as vague or as precise as you like. The last one set out above is a good one, as long as "readers" is not interpreted to mean every single reader (see myth 8). I think that, for all practical purposes, it makes *plain language* clear.

3. Plain language is not "text-based" rather than "reader-based"; it has always been concerned with whether the text works for readers and has long advocated testing on readers.

One old rap against plain language is that it concentrates on text instead of readers and testing documents on readers.[17] But the definition we just looked at favorably — a definition that is all about readers — should close the file on that charge.

---

[16] E-mail from Annetta Cheek to the author and others (Dec. 8, 2011) (recommending modest changes to the definition published in *Clarity*).

[17] *See* Robyn Penman, *Unspeakable Acts and Other Deeds: A Critique of Plain Legal Language*, 7 Information Design J. 121 (1993).

Historically, it may have been true that the criticism of legalese and officialese was mostly fueled by their unusual, not to say arcane and twisted, linguistic features. Thomas Jefferson, for instance, complained about the style of American statutes, "which, from their verbosity, their endless tautologies . . . and their multiplied efforts at certainty, by *said*s and *aforesaid*s, by *or*s and by *and*s, to make them more plain, are really rendered more perplexed and incomprehensible, not only to common readers, but to the lawyers themselves."[18] Yet notice: in the very sentence in which he complains about legal style, he concerns himself with its effect on readers. I'd posit that you will rarely find an indictment that doesn't explicitly or implicitly depend on how the text strikes readers and whether it's clear to them. How could it be otherwise? The criticism is not just that legalese and officialese are often silly and always unnecessary, but that they don't work. They frustrate, irritate, confuse, and defeat readers.

A similar point should be made about the advice and guidelines for writing in plain language. They aren't offered for some rarefied aesthetic purpose. They are ways to reach the ultimate goal of clarity — of readers' being able to find, understand, and use.

Emphatically, then: the supposed distinction between text-based and reader-based approaches is fanciful and false. They are inseparable.

That brings us to testing on readers. Almost from the beginning of the movement in the mid-1970s, plain-language advocates and organizations have been strongly on the side of testing. The influential Document Design Center stressed

---

[18] Thomas Jefferson, *The Writings of Thomas Jefferson* vol. 1, 65 (Andrew A. Lipscomb ed., Thomas Jefferson Memorial Ass'n of the U.S. 1904).

it 30 years ago.[19] In 1992, in the original version of my "Elements of Plain Language," I said, "Whenever possible, test consumer documents on a small group of typical users."[20] The literature is unequivocal on the value and importance of testing.[21]

So is actual practice. In part 5 of this book, you'll see that many of those studies involved documents that were improved through testing. And there are more on the way — far-reaching ones — from the U.S. government.

The new Consumer Financial Protection Bureau is authorized to develop plain-language disclosure forms that are "validated through consumer testing."[22] Elizabeth Warren, the acting director of the Bureau at its inception, had this to say about the drafts of its proposed mortgage-disclosure forms: "We will keep testing, adjusting, and retesting from the public and industry comments we receive until we get it right."[23] Participants in six cities will answer more than 60 questions to determine whether they can understand the basic

---

[19] *The Process Model of Document Design*, 18 Simply Stated (newsletter of American Institutes for Research) 1, 4 (July 1981) ("Before you can pronounce your document successful, you must find out — preferably by empirical testing — whether it *works*.").

[20] *Plain English: A Charter for Clear Writing*, *supra* n. 12, at 12.

[21] Asprey, *supra* n. 1, at 311–30 (describing the reasons for testing, projects that have involved testing, a number of informal testing methods, and nine formal methods); Martin Cutts, *The Oxford Guide to Plain English* 173–75, 198 (3d ed., Oxford U. Press 2009) (also describing many different methods); Robert D. Eagleson, *Writing in Plain English* 80–83 (Australian Gov't Publ'g Serv. 1990; repr. 1994) (the same); Neil James, *Writing at Work: How to Write Clearly, Effectively and Professionally* 23–29 (Allen & Unwin 2007) (the same).

[22] Dodd–Frank Wall Street Reform and Consumer Protection Act of 2010, Pub. L. No. 111-203, § 1032(b)(3), 124 Stat. 1376, 2007 (available at http://www.gpo.gov/fdsys/pkg/PLAW-111publ203/pdf/PLAW-111publ203.pdf).

[23] Gadi Dechter, *America's Next Top Model Disclosure*, http://thehill.com/blogs/congress-blog/politics/162897-Americasnext-top-model-disclosure (May 24, 2011).

terms of a mortgage offer and distinguish between competing offers.

Likewise, to help consumers understand their health-insurance coverage, the Department of Health and Human Services will require insurers to provide a new, standardized plain-English summary that was developed through a public process that included consumer testing.[24] That requirement takes effect in September 2012.

Testing has begun to take root, and success stories like these will continue to accumulate.

Now, the results of testing will obviously depend on many variables: the type of test, the complexity of the subject, the experience and ability of the readers, the skill of the writer or reviser, and more. And almost by definition, the degree of improvement on a revised document will depend on how well readers understood the original: the better the result, the less room there is for improvement. Finally, because there are limits to the level of comprehension we can expect with some documents, such as legal documents, our goals in testing must be reasonable. That said, even small improvements in mass public documents can produce huge savings in time and money.

But it's not always possible to formally test. There may not be the money or the inclination or the time. Much depends, obviously, on how often the document will be used and how many readers it will have. The greater the number of readers, the more compelling the case for testing because of the potential eye-popping benefits. Still, it's just not always in the cards.

So what should a writer do? The writer can still plan the document, that is, still treat it as part of a process. How? At least think about who will read the document, what the readers will have to do with it, what their motivation is, and

---

[24] http://www.hhs.gov/news/press/2012pres/02/20120209a.html (Feb. 9, 2012); *see also* http://www.usability.gov (providing information and resources to help with testing government websites for usability).

what knowledge and reading ability they have. Even do some informal testing by showing the proposed document to the client or a potential reader. Ask the client whether it carries out his or her wishes, or ask readers to mark parts that they don't understand or to write questions in the margins. This is the same kind of informal testing that the legal profession and government agencies do when they send out court rules and administrative regulations for comment. One expert describes it as the simplest of ten testing methods.[25]

In any event, the writer must at some point think about design and organization and style. Let's assume that he or she is not just ordering up the formbook or office model. Let's also assume that he or she has the training and skill needed to write in plain language. What should the writer do if it's not possible to bring any kind of testing to bear? What kinds of choices should the writer make?

Again, that's where part 5 of this book comes in. The empirical evidence is all on the side of plain language: compared with traditional style, it's not only strongly preferred but also much more likely to be read and understood and heeded — in much less time. In short, the guidelines that have been developed through research and experience will improve most legal and official documents. They are the writer's best bet — by far.

To put it another way, I challenge anyone to systematically violate plain-language guidelines and still produce clear, effective documents.

4. Plain language involves much more than just simple words and short sentences.

Some years ago, a letter-writer to the *Michigan Bar Journal*, sputtering about the "Plain English Jihad," proclaimed that he did "not look forward to a day of bland, two-syllable

---

[25] James, *supra* n. 21, at 23.

words and five-word sentences."[26] No doubt that misguided view still persists in some quarters. It echoes myth 1, and it takes to an extreme myth 3 — that plain language is "text-based" and concentrates on words and sentences. And with these misconceptions come all the arguments against text-based guidelines: long sentences can be managed with effective structure; a series of short sentences will be monotonous; there can be good reasons to use the passive voice; ceremonial language (*the truth, the whole truth, and nothing but the truth*) has its place; not all nominalizations (nouns that could be converted to verbs) should be replaced; an occasional extra word or sentence does not sink the ship; the guidelines may conflict with each other in a particular instance; shorter does not always mean clearer; writing is an art that requires judgment; readability formulas are only a measuring device, not a guarantee; and so on.

We know. These are nonissues. Every reputable book on plain language recognizes, for instance, the good uses of the passive voice.[27] Everyone recognizes that clarity may occasionally call for additional words in spots,[28] although a plain-language document will almost always be shorter overall. Any guideline is just that — a guideline, not an

---

[26] 73 Mich. B.J. 886 (1994).

[27] *See, e.g.*, Mark Adler, *Clarity for Lawyers: Effective Legal Writing* 98 (2d ed., The Law Society 2007); Cutts, *supra* n. 21, at 57–58; Eagleson, *supra* n. 21, at 47; Richard C. Wydick, *Plain English for Lawyers* 31 (5th ed., Carolina Academic Press 2005).

[28] *See, e.g.*, Robert C. Dick, *Legal Drafting in Plain Language* 23 (3d ed., Carswell 1995) ("Brevity does not necessarily breed clarity, although lean, terse language usually does clarify the contents of a document."); Wayne Schiess, *Better Legal Writing: 15 Topics for Advanced Legal Writers* 119 (William S. Hein & Co. 2005) ("[P]lain-English advocates reject pompous legalisms even if the everyday-English substitute is longer or requires more words.").

inflexible rule. But guidelines are still valuable, even indispensable.[29]

What's more — and this is the fundamental point — the guidelines for plain language are not narrowly circumscribed but instead range over planning, design, organization, sentences, words, and (yes) testing. And they number in the dozens. In part 2, I listed 42. Bryan Garner lists 50.[30] Judge Mark Painter lists 40.[31] The U.S. federal-government plain-language website lists about 45.[32] Martin Cutts lists 25, most of them with a number of subpoints.[33] And so it is with other books and resources on plain language: sentences and words are an important part of the picture, but only a part.

It's true, of course, that not every voice in the choir sounds exactly the same; that some articles and advocates are more narrowly focused than others; and that casual observers, including many lawyers, still think plain language is all about vocabulary, or getting rid of archaic words and complex verbiage. It's also true, as noted earlier, that the very term *plain language* lends itself to a narrow interpretation. But that interpretation is not accurate, not if you listen to the full choir.

---

[29] *See* Janice C. Redish & Susan Rosen, *Can Guidelines Help Writers?* in *Plain Language: Principles and Practice* 83, 86–87 (Erwin R. Steinberg ed., Wayne State U. Press 1991) (noting that "[g]uidelines distill research and good practice into chunks of useful advice" and that all writers use guidelines whether they realize it or not — either explicit guidelines or ones they have internalized).

[30] Bryan A. Garner, *Legal Writing in Plain English* (U. Chicago Press 2001).

[31] Mark Painter, *40 Rules for the Art of Legal Writing* (4th ed., Jarndyce & Jarndyce Press 2009).

[32] *Federal Plain-Language Guidelines*, http://www.plainlanguage.gov (rev. May 2011).

[33] Cutts, *supra* n. 21.

5. Regardless of what readers may expect in legal and official documents, they certainly prefer plain language.

Some might argue that readers expect to see legalese and officialese in those kinds of documents. Increasingly, that's not true: "the era when clients will accept and pay for legal documents that they cannot understand — and are not expected to understand — is fading away."[34]

But this argument, or excuse, is cold comfort to apologists in any case. To the extent that readers still expect to see legalese and officialese, then shame on the writers who have conditioned them to expect it — because readers don't *want* to see anything of the sort. And they say so in one survey after another. In 1992, I cited two surveys of the public with numbers like these:

- 64% said they are frustrated when they read legal documents.
- 57% said that legal documents are poorly written and hard to read.
- 33% said that lawyers don't even try to communicate with the average person — the lowest rating received by any profession in the survey.
- 48% said government and business forms are too complicated.

---

[34] Schiess, *supra* n. 1, at 53; *see also* Asprey, *supra* n. 1, at 45 ("It used to be thought that clients expect their lawyers to write in legalese and would be disappointed if they didn't. Those days are receding fast . . . ."); Bryan A. Garner, *Securities Disclosure in Plain English* 4 (Commerce Clearing House 1999) ("Clients — especially sophisticated clients — are demanding more from their lawyers. They know now that they ought to be able to read and understand their wills, their leases, and their other contracts.").

- 58% stopped using the service or organization that provided the form, or gave up trying to fill it out.[35]

Likewise, in a 2004 "Perplexity Poll" by the Siegel+Gale firm:

- 36% could not correctly answer a question about using the cholesterol drug Lipitor from the product-information sheet.
- 43% could not correctly answer a question about Medicare Part B from the benefits form.
- Of the persons who had purchased a product for $50 or more within 30 days and had to contact the manufacturer or retailer for help, 72% cited the lack of clear, understandable instructions as the primary reason; 34% of those were not satisfied with the help; and 70% of those who were not satisfied said they would definitely not purchase another product from that manufacturer or retailer.[36]

Siegel+Gale followed with another "Simplicity Survey" in 2009, and the results were more of the same:

- 65% of customers find investment prospectuses to be extremely difficult to understand.
- 50% find their insurance, credit-card, and cellphone contracts extremely or somewhat difficult to understand.
- From 32% to 52% sometimes or never read those materials.

---

[35] *Plain English: A Charter for Clear Writing, supra* n. 12, at 23–24 (reporting on surveys by the Plain Language Institute, in Vancouver, British Columbia, and the Document Design Center, in Washington, D.C.).

[36] *Perplexity Poll: Americans Befuddled by Business Documents and Health Care Communications* 2 (Aug. 2004).

- 75% think that complexity and lack of understanding played a significant role in the worldwide financial crisis.

- A stunning 84% are more likely to trust a company that uses jargon-free language in its communications.[37]

These numbers dull the senses, but their import is unmistakable: readers of public and legal documents detest complexity and crave simplicity. And these preferences are borne out by the before-and-after studies summarized in the second half of part 5. We have empirically tested — up one side and down the other — this question of reader preferences and comprehension. Every law student, every lawyer, every government writer, every business writer, and everyone else who can influence public communication needs to know about this body of evidence. It demolishes all the rationalizations for traditional style except three: I didn't have the will, the skill, or the time to do better.

6. There is time to write in plain language — or at least to make a serious start.

You can point to an assortment of reasons why writers resist or dismiss plain language, but I think they come down to the three just mentioned: lack of will, lack of skill, and lack of time. I'll get back to lack of time in just a moment.

Lack of will has its own fairly obvious causes. One is pure inertia, admittedly a powerful force. It's usually easier to do things the old way — to copy an old form, for instance,

---

[37] *Simplicity Survey: A Clarion Call for Transparency* 2, 3 (Jan. 2009); *see also* Securities & Exchange Comm'n, *Toward Greater Transparency* 3 (2009) (available at http://www.sec.gov/spotlight/disclosureinitiative/report.pdf) (noting that respondents in a survey about disclosure documents had difficulty with their jargon and length and with finding information — making the time required "too burdensome for many other than the professional investor").

or to fall back on jargon. Another cause is a false notion of power and prestige, of being in control, of having the status conferred by a mysterious and seemingly magical language. Yet another is a belief in the very myths addressed in this part of the book, along with a profoundly misplaced confidence in traditional style — by writers who must not realize how ineffective, inefficient, unnecessary, and prone to uncertainty that style is.

Not many writers would own up to a paralysis induced by those causes. As Robert Benson put it almost 30 years ago in a brilliant article, "These motivations lack any intellectually or socially acceptable rationale; they amount to assertions of naked self-interest."[38]

Even fewer writers would admit to a lack of skill. In fact, though, judges do not give high marks to the briefs they read, briefs that prompt a "strong, recurring, and unmistakable cry for conciseness and clarity."[39] Lawyers themselves estimate that only 5% of the documents they read are well drafted (although, in a triumph of self-deception, 95% of them would claim to produce high-quality documents).[40] Of course, the only remedy for lack of skill is education and training — in the schools and afterward, throughout a writer's professional life. Otherwise, we may never see and guard against the flaws

---

[38] Benson, *supra* n. 1, at 571.

[39] *See* Kristin K. Robbins, *The Inside Scoop: What Federal Judges Really Think About the Way Lawyers Write*, 8 Legal Writing: J. Legal Writing Inst. 257, 268, 276, 279 (2002) (reporting that only 23% of 355 judges surveyed rated the analysis in briefs as very good or excellent, only 11% gave that rating to the writing style, and only 19% said the briefs were usually concise).

[40] Bryan A. Garner, *President's Letter*, The Scrivener (newsletter of Scribes — American Society of Legal Writers) 1, 3 (Winter 1998) (reporting on Garner's survey of lawyers at his seminars); *see also* Carl Felsenfeld, *The Plain English Movement in the United States*, 6 Canadian Business L.J. 408, 413 (1981–1982) ("Lawyers have two common failings. One is that they do not write well and the other is that they think they do.").

in what we have to read. They will become our own bad habits.

That brings us back to lack of time, or a perceived lack of time. This is the reason that writers would probably cite most often for not embracing change or not doing better on a particular piece of work. And it has some validity — but not a lot. No doubt all professional writers are pressed for time, but that should not prevent them from at least making a start. How hard would it be to do a global computer search for *prior to* and *pursuant to*, or for the *here-*, *there-*, and *where-* words? How hard would it be for lawyers to stop beginning their complaints with *NOW COMES* and ending affidavits with *Further affiant sayeth naught*? If nothing else, writers can pick off some of the prime offenders.

Then writers could move to full standard documents, starting with the most important or common ones they deal with. Work on those documents one at a time. If the supervisor is involved, ask for permission to try an experiment. I know of one young lawyer, working in a prosecutor's office, who took it upon himself to do just that and wound up revising dozens of office forms over the next year.

For documents that are not form documents but are written from scratch, even the demands of time should not excuse some things. Benson again:

> [A] good writer — or a good lawyer — should not panic or flail about under pressure, grabbing onto . . . 100-word sentences, illogical organization, and the absurd medieval style of legalese, for comfort. A good lawyer — one who deserves to earn a paycheck for practicing this craft — will admit occasional compromises with reality, but will maintain level-headed writing and thinking under pressure.[41]

---

[41] Benson, *supra* n. 1, at 568.

Yes, writers are pressed for time. But rarely are they so intensely pressed that they don't have time to think, outline, organize, and attend to the prose. They might not have time to make it perfect. But they are never justified in lapsing into the worst linguistic habits of their professions.

7. **The push for plain language will not result in less work and less prestige for lawyers; it could even produce more work, and it will surely improve their image.**

Talk about naked self-interest — it's one strange argument that writing plainly will hurt the legal profession financially. I've heard it, though.

What does this argument boil down to? That we lawyers want to persist in our hocus-pocus so that we can keep people under our sway — a kind of keep-'em-dumb theory? That we have a vested interest in obscurity, in clouding every law and legal paper with impenetrable legalese? That we owe it to our fellow lawyers to keep writing documents — an offer to sell a house, say, or a service contact — that a buyer will have to take to another lawyer to interpret? (Never mind that many times the other lawyer won't understand it either.[42])

This whole notion is deeply cynical and even unethical. We cannot and should not expect to fool people forever. Obedience based on ignorance may work for a while but will eventually lead to disrespect and contempt. I'm sure most lawyers realize that, and I think very few of them, when pressed, would argue for deliberate obscurity. There's no vast conspiracy to perpetuate legalese. It keeps its hold on many lawyers, sadly, for the reasons discussed in the previous section (inertia, habit, overreliance on old models, a

---

[42] *See* Law Reform Comm'n of Victoria, *supra* n. 1, at 17 ("Many legal documents . . . are unintelligible to the ordinary reader, and barely intelligible to many lawyers.").

misunderstanding of plain language, lack of training and self-awareness, and the specter of too little time).

Rather than being a financial disadvantage, plain language presents an opportunity to gain a competitive edge. Lawyers and law firms can distinguish themselves through the clarity of their communications. That has actually happened, especially in Australia, where leading firms began to market plain-language legal services in the mid-1980s and where that practice is now described as "mainstream."[43] Two examples:

- Mallesons Stephen Jaques set up an interoffice committee, ran a comprehensive training program, created almost 200 plain-language business documents, sold some of the documents to different clients, and used them to attract new clients to the firm.[44]
- Phillips Fox "attracted new clients — including life offices, insurers, manufacturers, a bank, and a major government department — all of which came to the firm because of its commitment to plain language."[45]

I wonder what would happen if firms elsewhere decided to market an ability to write to and for their clients in the plain, clear style that all readers — lawyers included — strongly prefer.

Besides, any financial calculation has to take into account the considerable costs and inefficiencies of legalese for everyone involved: the extra time to read it and try to figure it out, the extra time for lawyers to explain what they've written to clients, and the costs of having to deal with and fix mistakes. Mark Adler gives several telling examples from his years in practice and says this:

---

[43] Asprey, *supra* n. 1, at 47.

[44] Edward Kerr, *Using Plain Language in Law Firms*, 73 Mich. B.J. 48 (Jan. 1994).

[45] Mark Duckworth & Christopher Balmford, *Convincing Business That Clarity Pays*, 73 Mich. B.J. 1314, 1315 (Dec. 1994).

[J]ust as a traditional document takes even longer to understand than its unnecessary length would lead us to expect, so will it contain disproportionately more mistakes. Legalese breeds many errors that could be avoided by clear expression.[46]

Perhaps lawyers who buy into the I-profit-from-legalese argument are concerned that forms mills will capture some of their business. But legal forms have always been widely available in office-supply stores, in libraries, from service providers (like real-estate agents), even from bar associations (the American Bar Association offers a medical power of attorney). Is there a concern that forms in plain language are especially attractive and thus a heightened danger to profitability? Really? I doubt that many business clients or consumers who would otherwise hire a lawyer to draft a commercial lease or a trust would suddenly start turning to new plain-language forms if they became readily available. And to the extent that people can sensibly — big word: sensibly — use forms for routine, uncomplicated legal matters, so be it:

There may come a utopian time when all our precedents [forms] are clearly written and fewer lawyers will be needed; if so, let the least talented aspiring newcomers choose a career more useful than stoking fog.[47]

Stoking fog. Justice Holmes is said to have used a similar figure: "Lawyers spend a great deal of their time shoveling smoke."[48] Isn't this the image that much of the public has of lawyers? Put aside the dubious argument about financial detriment. Then think about the ridicule and disrespect caused by the funny way lawyers write and talk. There *is* a remedy. Bryan Garner: "If we [lawyers] want the respect of the public,

---

[46] Adler, *supra* n. 27, at 10.

[47] *Id.* at 7.

[48] Quoted in Bryan A. Garner, *Judges on Effective Writing: The Importance of Plain Language*, 84 Mich. B.J. 44, 44 (Feb. 2005).

we must learn to communicate simply and directly."[49] Robert
Eagleson: "If lawyers would improve their image, increase
their proficiency, and sharpen their competitive edge, they
must get rid of gobbledygook from legal language."[50]

Legalese shares with officialese a terrible failing: it puts
people off, leaves them cold. In varying degrees, its tone is
highfalutin, fusty, impersonal, and sometimes inhuman, as if
cranked out of a machine. No wonder that readers so dislike
it, and in turn tend to dislike any group it's associated with.

8. Proponents do not imagine that plain language will be intelligible to everyone; they do expect writers to make documents intelligible to the greatest possible number of intended readers.

It bears repeating that our goals for legal and official documents must be reasonable and will vary with the document.
Not everyone is going to understand even a plain one, no
matter how proficient the writer or how careful the process.

Let's back up to the definition endorsed earlier, which is
stated in terms of whether the "*intended readers* can easily
find what they need, understand it, and use it." Realistically,
or implicitly, that means the *great majority* of the intended
readers, whose backgrounds and motivation may vary
considerably. At the same time, since there may be more than
one group of readers — more than one audience — writers
should not constrict their view of the intended readers.
Normally, they should write for the primary or immediate
readers (and sometimes, if need be, even write another
document for a secondary audience). While the primary
audience can sometimes be hard to describe, most often it's
not.

---

[49] Garner, *supra* n. 6, at 680.

[50] Robert D. Eagleson, *Plain English — A Boon for Lawyers*, The Second
Draft (newsletter of Legal Writing Inst.) 12, 13 (Oct. 1991).

In law, though, a constricted view has settled in. The attitude among many drafters of statutes, rules, contracts, and the like is that they should draft primarily for the judge who might someday have to interpret those legal instruments. That's so misguided. First, only a tiny percentage of documents — far less than 1% — are ever litigated. Second, drafting primarily for the judge (whatever that means) discounts everyone else affected by the document, including those who administer it and the citizens it governs. Do we not care about administrative ease and efficiency? Do we dismiss citizens as merely secondary or as incapable of delving into such priestly matters? Third, as already noted, legalese is *more* likely than plain language to cause mistakes and uncertainty, not less likely. And this will in turn be more likely to engender disputes and litigation that never should have happened in the first place:

> [T]he further removed a document is from plain English, the more you'll get divergent views on its meaning — even from judges. . . . If you write well for the front-end users, you're less likely to have trouble down the line.[51]

Here's the better view of what drafters should aim for when writing for the public at large:

> The plain-English movement does not require that laws always be drafted in such a way as to make them intelligible to the average citizen. However, it does require that every effort be made to make them intelligible to the widest possible audience. There is no justification for . . . defects in language and structure . . . which sharply reduce the range of people who are capable of comprehending a document.[52]

Nobody imagines that plain language will obviate the need for lawyers or legal services or citizens' guides to law.

---

[51] Garner, *supra* n. 30, at 91, 93.
[52] Law Reform Comm'n of Victoria, *supra* n. 1, at 51.

Nobody claims that it squeezes out all the uncertainty and never leaves room for interpretation. Nor does anybody doubt that making statutes and regulations more intelligible to nonlawyers is a challenge and that gains are sometimes modest. But enlightened drafters still recognize their obligation to take up the challenge:

> Acts of Parliament (and regulations too) are consulted and used by a large number of people who are not lawyers.... Many ... people ... refer to legislation in their jobs. People who work in the registries of universities ... make constant reference to educational legislation; employers and trade union officials need to be well versed in employment legislation; the staff of many government departments . . . work closely with the legislation that their departments administer; the staff of local authorities need to access . . . local government legislation; and company officers need to consult company and financial reporting legislation. At other times, ordinary people refer to Acts of Parliament to find the answers to problems that affect them in their personal lives [examples omitted].[53]

Even apart from their own drafting, lawyers' attitudes affect the goal of greater intelligibility in another way. There's an old refrain among consultants and technical writers who work to produce a new document for a company or agency: the legal department killed it or mutilated it.

> I am a technical writer, not a lawyer.... I have taught clear writing principles to numerous people from both business and government.... What I find sort of funny is that, universally, the people I teach say that they understand all the points I make and try to write this way, but that their documents become full of meaningless jargon, poor construction, and passive voice

---

[53] New Zealand Law Comm'n, Report 104, *Presentation of New Zealand Statute Law* 14–15 (Oct. 2008) (available at http://lawcom.govt.nz/project/presentation-new-zealand-statute-law).

after they go through their legal departments. No doubt this is not true for everyone, but I'm afraid that lawyers do have a fairly bad rep in the technical writing community.[54]

Naturally, if any reason is even given for the lawyers' pushback, the reason has vaguely to do with legal necessity or legal accuracy (see myth 10).

One expert tells about redesigning forms for New York City's Department of Transportation. After a careful process involving four drafts (you should see the difference between the old and new forms), "the legal team derailed the project."[55] The lawyers were concerned that the revision "did not use the same legal language as the original."[56] Close-mindedness strikes again.

That's not to say writers might better go it alone. On any project, experts in the particular field should of course be involved, ideally as part of a team formed at the beginning. Then how does the writer proceed?

First of all, try to create an atmosphere of mutual respect. On a lengthy project, work through a trial piece and establish a process.[57] Show that you know your stuff. Provide examples of plain language.[58] If you're told that a certain term or formulation is legally required, kindly ask for a citation to a case. Possibly check to see whether the case really requires that language or merely interprets how it applies in one set of circumstances. Be especially suspicious of the claim that

---

[54] Jim Collins, *Letter to the Editor*, 97 ABA J. 6 (Aug. 2011).

[55] Karen Schriver, *The Rhetoric of Redesign in Bureaucratic Settings*, in *¿Qué es el diseño de información?* (*What Is Information Design?*) 156, 163 (Jorge Frascara ed., Ediciones Infinito 2011) (available from Schriver at kschriver@earthlink.net).

[56] *Id.*

[57] Cheryl Stephens, *Working with Lawyers on Your Projects*, 66 Clarity 11, 12 (Nov. 2011) (stressing, among other good advice, the importance of a work plan).

[58] *Id.*

the language is required by statute.[59] Be politic but persistent — or as persistent as you can be without risking a project that might still make a difference or risking your job. And feel free to copy this and the previous two pages (or recommend this book).

The trouble is that the project may just go to the legal department and die. Perhaps some lawyers are too arrogant or embarrassed to even listen. Or they believe in myths. Or they are unskilled. Or they simply don't care whether the public can understand the company's or agency's documents. None of these reasons has anything to commend it.

9. Plain language is not subverted by the need to use technical terms.

A simple fact punctures overblown claims about the obstacle posed by technical terms: they are a tiny part of most legal and official documents. And that's true no matter how you look at them.

Consider terms of art, which are technical terms that convey in a word or two a fairly settled, precise meaning in a field: *plaintiff*, *bailment*, *felony*. In law, the best estimates are that they number "fewer than a hundred."[60] So some legal documents will not include a single term of art.

One commentator responds that technical terms include all those looser, seemingly ordinary words — like *reasonable care* and *malice* — whose "legal meaning is not contained or

---

[59] George Hathaway, *The Search for Legalese "Required by Statute,"* 69 Mich. B.J. 1286 (Dec. 1990) (pointing out that statutes requiring that certain information be given do not usually require specific wording).

[60] Garner, *supra* n. 5, at 193; *see also* Robert W. Benson, *Plain English Comes to Court*, 13 Litigation 21, 24 (Fall 1986) (likewise asserting that the list "surely" does not exceed 100); Stanley M. Johanson, *In Defense of Plain Language*, 3 Scribes J. Legal Writing 37, 39 (1992) (noting "the small subcategory comprising terms of art").

exhausted in their linguistic meaning."[61] Thus, the argument goes, specialized knowledge is required for a full understanding of a term like *possession* and whether it "includes situations in which the object is not physically possessed."[62] True enough, and if a passenger in a car is charged with "possessing" marijuana found in the trunk, the passenger needs to hire a lawyer. That doesn't mean the word *possess* in a statute makes it unplain or underdeveloped, or the term *good cause* in an employment contract, or *sound mind* in a will. Terms like these — which indeed are common in law (see myth 10) — will still be clear in most of their applications, and trying to cover every application is hardly sensible.

Besides that, even under the most expansive view of technical terms as including any terms that have been litigated, they remain just a sprinkling in the much larger mix. One notable study of a real-estate sales contract found that less than 3% of the words had significant legal meaning based on precedent.[63] This hardly puts a damper on plain language.

When a writer does need to use a technical term, then he or she should consider whether to explain or define it, or provide examples. This decision on how much detail to include is probably the toughest call in drafting. It often depends on who the intended readers are and how difficult or unusual the term is. You would not define *indemnify* in a commercial contract between business parties. But you probably should in a consumer contract, such as a car rental.

This advice is supported by part of a recent study. Lay readers were asked for their preference between two choices that might appear in a letter:

---

[61] Rabeea Assy, *Can the Law Speak Directly to Its Subjects? The Limitations of Plain Language,* 38 J. Law & Society 376, 400 (2011).

[62] *Id.* at 401.

[63] Benson Barr et al., *Legalese and the Myth of Case Precedent,* 64 Mich. B.J. 1136, 1137 (Oct. 1985).

(1) If you don't respond, the court will issue a default judgment.

(2) If you don't respond, the court will issue a default judgment. That means you'll lose, and the court will give the plaintiff what he is asking for.[64]

Just over 78% preferred the latter, even though it's obviously longer. And that result was consistent across all educational levels.

In any event, even a document that contains a few technical terms can be written in plain language. Advocates have been doing it for decades all around the world — as witness the many examples in parts 4 and 5. And they have been doing it on major projects involving important, complex subjects.

10. Plain language is not imprecise; in fact, it's more precise than traditional legal and official style.

This is the biggest myth, the grossest canard, the worst of all the misinformation about plain language. I've addressed it,[65] and so have others. The most thorough scholarly study of legal language was done by David Mellinkoff in his classic book, *The Language of the Law*. He said and proved that the argument from precision (in defense of traditional legal style) is the most "spurious" one of all.[66] Other experts agree:

- "Modern, plain English is as capable of precision as traditional legal English. It can cope with all the concepts and complexities of the law and legal

---

[64] Christopher R. Trudeau, *The Public Speaks: An Empirical Study of Legal Communication*, 14 Scribes J. Legal Writing ___ (forthcoming 2012).

[65] *The Great Myth That Plain Language Is Not Precise*, in *Lifting the Fog of Legalese*, *supra* n. 2, at 37.

[66] Mellinkoff, *supra* n. 1, at 290–398, 454.

processes. The few technical terms that the lawyer might feel compelled to retain for convenience or necessity can be incorporated without destroying the document's legal integrity."[67]

- "Using plain language does not mean giving up legal precision. Plain language can be at least as precise as traditional legal language."[68]

- "Anyone who challenges plain English on precision ought to carry out the exercise I just did [using a traditional phrase and a plainer equivalent]. Do the research. Look up the words in a legal-usage dictionary. Consult *Words and Phrases*. Then figure out if the legal word is really more precise than the ordinary word. Usually, it's not."[69]

The whole debate on this issue assumes, obviously, that traditional writing — especially legal writing — is precise to begin with. And that's a highly dubious assumption. More from the experts:

- "For this redundancy — for the accumulation of excrementitious matter in all its various shapes . . . — for all the pestilential effects that cannot but be produced by this so enormous a load of literary garbage, — the plea commonly pleaded . . . is, that it is necessary to *precision* — or, to use the word which on similar occasions [drafters] themselves are in the habit of using, *certainty*. But a more absolutely sham plea never was . . . pleaded . . . ."[70]

---

[67] Peter Butt & Richard Castle, *Modern Legal Drafting: A Guide to Using Clearer Language* 126 (2d ed., Cambridge U. Press 2006) (citation omitted).

[68] Asprey, *supra* n. 1, at 62.

[69] Schiess, *supra* n. 28, at 126.

[70] Jeremy Bentham, *The Works of Jeremy Bentham* vol. 3, 260 (John Bowring ed., Russell & Russell ca. 1843; repr. 1962).

- "The truth is that many people, lawyers included, buy into the fallacy that there must be a great deal of precision in legalese. . . . There is all too little precision in legal language, as many entries in this book should demonstrate."[71]
- "[T]here is relatively little precision, intelligible or unintelligible, in legal language."[72]

A corollary to the precision claim is the honed-by-precedent claim: the idea that legal language has been carefully shaped and refined by countless decisions over time. Any truth to this? Not much, says Mark Adler:

> The late Professor David Mellinkoff . . . found more than 2,000 citations of the word *accident* in [the resource *Words and Phrases*]. Does that mean it is now precise (but wasn't after the first 1,999 cases)? Or that it is now much more precise than it used to be, but still needs some litigation which your client offers to fund? . . . A moment's thought undermines the honing argument even without recourse to the details. Every case is decided on its own facts, and the decision will reflect the evidence . . . of the circumstances surrounding this particular use of the word, and in particular of the parties' intentions.[73]

Right. As noted earlier (with the *highway* example), all natural language is vague or indeterminate at some point, and the law abounds with terms that are exceptionally vague: *good cause, probable cause, proximate cause, negligent, gross negligence, willful, beyond* [a party's] *control, genuine issue*

---

[71] Garner, *supra* n. 6, at 595, 596.

[72] Benson, *supra* n. 1, at 560.

[73] Adler, *supra* n. 27, at 9; *see also* Mark Adler, *Tried and Tested: The Myth Behind the Cliché*, 34 Clarity 45, 50 (Jan. 1996) (examining a typically verbose repair clause in a lease, along with cases interpreting similar clauses, and concluding that (1) the "torrential style" did not help the drafters and (2) the cases provide no rational basis for the verbose wording).

of material fact (doubly vague), *probable, relevant, substantial, sufficient, irreparable, unfair prejudice, undue influence, unjust enrichment, due process, reasonable doubt, reasonable* this, *reasonable* that. The list goes on. And borderline cases are inevitable. Judges and lawyers manage to deal with them using different interpretive aids (analogy, canons of construction, policy, social context, and others). Yet the fact remains: the law is not and never has been so very precise, even at its best, even apart from its unnecessary obscurity and complexity, even apart from legalese.

Nobody doubts that legal writers need to aim for accuracy and the right measure of precision. We might even say that the goal should be a "precisely appropriate degree of imprecision"[74] — to create whatever flexibility is needed. But the search for absolute precision is a pipe dream, and it's often self-defeating as well because it encourages writers to overload the document with remote contingencies, unnecessary detail, and repetitions that foster inconsistency. Thus, besides being virtually unavoidable, vagueness has its advantages.

In any case, the choice between precision and clarity is usually a false choice. If anything, plain language is *more* precise than traditional legal and official writing because it uncovers the ambiguities and gaps and errors that traditional style, with all its excesses, tends to hide. So not only is plain language the great clarifier, it improves the substance as well.

Want proof? Ask the people in organizations that have undertaken plain-language projects. They will routinely tell you that they were surprised, and sometimes terrified, by the deficiencies they discovered in their trusted old documents. They will tell you that the process of revising into plain language revealed all kinds of unnecessary and overlapping substance. They will tell you that the final product was clearer, more readable, more consistent, *and* more accurate. Here, again, is a small sampling of testimonials:

---

[74] Charles P. Curtis, *It's Your Law* 76 (Harvard U. Press 1954).

- "The first contracts in simple English received considerable publicity.... Even a superficial comparison of the new versions to the older counterparts should have led people to realize that language was only part of the improvement. Simplicity was made possible through a reduction in substance."[75]
- "[T]he rewriting process inevitably uncovers ambiguities and, at least in the [federal] appellate rules . . . , ambiguities which had never been litigated and never been resolved."[76]
- "The [rewriting] process, although very detailed and time-consuming, was most enlightening. I do not mind admitting that, on a couple of occasions during the rewrite, I was a little embarrassed by the . . . frequently absurd and *occasionally wrong* documents on which we base our whole operation."[77]
- "A few years ago I was part of a team developing a plain lease that a major organization decided to introduce for its clients . . . . Clause 12 read [details omitted]. Two major legal firms responded angrily on behalf of their clients [that the clause was "absolutely unacceptable" and "an unreasonable fetter" on their clients]. We politely reminded the lawyers of the corresponding clause 14 in the earlier versions of the lease, which they had allowed their clients to sign each year for the past 20 years."[78]

---

[75] Carl Felsenfeld & Alan Siegel, *Writing Contracts in Plain English* 48 (West Publ'g Co. 1981).

[76] Carol Ann T. Mooney, *Simplification of the [Federal] Rules of [Appellate] Procedure*, 105 Dickinson L. Rev. 237, 239 (2001).

[77] Christopher Balmford, *Lawyers, About-Face: As Plain as You Like*, 90 Mich. B.J. 58, 59 (Aug. 2011) (quoting the national manager for a major Australian life-insurance company).

[78] Robert Eagleson, *Plain Language: Changing the Lawyer's Image and Goals*, 7 Scribes J. Legal Writing 119, 137 (1998–2000).

Now, there's a game played by doubters and critics. They will scrutinize a plain-language project to try to find some place where you might possibly, arguably, conceivably have changed the meaning or not gotten the meaning right. See, they'll say, plain language doesn't work. You made a mistake. Never mind that you probably fixed a bunch of uncertainties and cleared up heaps of confusion in the original. Never mind that the plain-language version is ten times better. Never mind that the mistake, if it's serious enough and wasn't caught during the process, can likely be fixed through an amendment. Here's what the Law Reform Commission of Victoria said about one of its projects:

> If some detail has been missed, it could readily be included without affecting the style of the plain English version. It would not be necessary to resort to the convoluted and repetitious style of the original, nor to introduce the unnecessary concepts which it contains. Any errors in the plain English version are the result of difficulties of translation, particularly difficulties in understanding the original version. They are not inherent in plain English itself. Ideally, of course, plain English should not involve a translation. It should be written from the beginning.[79]

The irony is that while critics will bend over backwards to find a flaw in a plain-language document, they typically don't or won't apply the same scrutiny and standards to old-style documents. If they did, they might feel rather deflated. I've tried to make this point with my own work on the U.S. federal court rules — by providing scores of side-by-side examples from the old and new Federal Rules of Civil Procedure[80] and identifying dozens of deficiencies in each of

---

[79] *Plain English and the Law, supra* n. 1, at 49.

[80] *Lessons in Drafting from the New Federal Rules of Civil Procedure*, 12 Scribes J. Legal Writing 25 (2008–2009) (available at http://www.uscourts.gov/uscourts/RulesAndPolicies/rules/Style%20Resources/Lessons%20in%20Drafting.pdf).

some random examples from the old Federal Rules of Evidence.[81]

How many more times do proponents have to do this? How many more revisions and demonstrations will it take to make the case? Isn't 50 years' worth of myth-busting — going back to Mellinkoff — enough?

In the end, you have to wonder just what it is that traditionalists are defending about traditional style. And you have to wonder whether they have had the slightest experience with plain language or given a moment's thought to what it can accomplish.

Read on.

---

[81] *Drafting Examples from the Proposed New Federal Rules of Evidence,* 80 Mich. B.J. 52 (Aug. 2009), 46 (Sept. 2009), 54 (Oct. 2009), 50 (Nov. 2009) (available at http://www.michbar.org/generalinfo/plainenglish/ columns.cfm); *see also* Mark Cooney, *Style Is Substance: Collected Cases Showing Why It Matters,* 14 Scribes J. Legal Writing 1 (forthcoming 2012) (collecting about 45 cases that turned on or criticized some aspect of the lawyers' writing, such as legalese, verbosity, convoluted sentences, ill-advised passives, and ambiguity); *Examples of Plain Language,* http://www.plainlanguage.gov/testExamples/index.cfm (containing many before-and-after examples from government writing).

PART FOUR

Some Historical Highlights

This part is mainly for the historical record but also for fun. Nobody has tried to assemble a collection quite like this — which should demonstrate the depth and range and concrete results of worldwide efforts to promote plain language for half a century. And I hope readers will enjoy the retrospective. For plain-language veterans, it should evoke good memories and a feeling of accomplishment. For relative newcomers, perhaps it will serve as an inspiration of sorts. Even though some things have come and gone, they all added to the gathering international force.

Of course, any list of highlights is bound to raise eyebrows over what is and isn't included. I did solicit opinions, weighed all the suggestions, and even presented the tentative list at an international conference. But in the end, it's not meant to be complete or definitive. Certainly, there are — and have been — other important publications, laws, events, organizations, and consultancies.

For almost all the summaries, I tried to identify the people who were closest to the events and enlist their help. Without exception, they kindly agreed to draft or help draft a summary, so this part 4 includes the work of 34 contributors. To all of them, named on the next page, I'm very grateful.

Ruth Baldwin
Christopher Balmford
Candice Burt
Peter Butt
Halton Cheadle
Annetta Cheek
Martin Cutts
Gwen Davies
Bill DuBay
Mark Duckworth
Gail Dykstra
Robert Eagleson
Barbro Ehrenberg-Sundin
David Elliott
Nicole Fernbach
Malcolm Gammie
Lynda Harris

Anne-Marie Hasselrot
Debra Huron
Kenneth Keith
Anne Kjærgaard
Margrethe Kvarenes
Eamonn Moran
Sissel Motzfeldt
Christine Mowat
Eva Olovsson
Aino Piehl
Ginny Redish
Torunn Reksten
Ann Scott
Jóhannes B. Sigtryggsson
Nancy Smith
Cheryl Stephens
Emma Wagner

PUBLICATIONS

1. U.S.: David Mellinkoff's Book *The Language of the Law*

Criticism of legal writing goes back more than four centuries.[1] But Mellinkoff's book, published in 1963, gave scholarly weight — and undeniable validity — to those criticisms, thus providing the intellectual foundation for the plain-language movement in law. The book traced the history of English legal language back to the time of the Celts, before the birth of Christ. Mellinkoff concluded that legal language has a strong tendency to be "wordy, unclear, pompous, and dull."[2] He famously said that "the principle of simplicity would dictate that the language used by lawyers agree with the common speech, unless there are reasons for a difference."[3] And in the second half of the book, he disposed of — through careful analysis and countless examples — the supposed reasons why legal language should or must be different from ordinary English. He called the argument from precision the most "spurious" of them all.[4]

2. U.S.: Richard Wydick's Book *Plain English for Lawyers*

In 1979, there appeared the first edition of a slim book — 93 pages — called *Plain English for Lawyers*, by Richard Wydick.

---

[1] *See* Joseph Kimble, *Lifting the Fog of Legalese: Essays on Plain Language* appendix 1 (Carolina Academic Press 2006).

[2] *The Language of the Law* 24 (Little Brown & Co. 1963).

[3] *Id.* at vii.

[4] *Id.* at 454.

It opened, memorably, like this:

> We lawyers do not write plain English. We use
> eight words to say what could be said in two. We use
> arcane phrases to express commonplace ideas. Seeking
> to be precise, we become redundant. Seeking to be
> cautious, we become verbose. Our sentences twist on,
> phrase within clause within clause, glazing the eyes
> and numbing the minds of our readers.[5]

Wydick then went on to boldly tell us — and show us
how — to omit surplus words; use strong verbs, not noun
forms; prefer the active voice; use short sentences, on average;
arrange words with care; choose familiar, concrete words and
cut out the silly lawyerisms; and avoid various language
quirks. By now, this is pretty familiar advice — thanks in
large part to this book. Its fresh tone, lively style, and very
compactness made the lessons stick.

Plain English for Lawyers is in its fifth edition. It's still a
slim book, at 128 pages. There are 800,000 copies in print. It
has guided and changed lawyers and law students for more
than 30 years. No other book on legal writing can match that
claim.

3. U.S.: "Plain Language" Column in the *Michigan Bar Journal*

In 1981, the State Bar of Michigan formed a Plain-English
Committee, composed of judges and lawyers who served
voluntarily. Over the years, the committee produced a
videotape called *Everything You Wanted to Know About
Legalese . . . But Were Afraid to Ask*, gave Clarity Awards
for well-written documents throughout the 1990s, and
worked on a number of forms projects.

In 1984, the committee also began producing a monthly
"Plain Language" column for the *Michigan Bar Journal*. The

---

[5] *Plain English for Lawyers* 3 (5th ed., Carolina Academic Press 2005).

committee itself was discontinued in 2001 but left the column as its enduring legacy. It's the longest-running legal-writing column anywhere, a rich source for the theory and practice of plain writing. A chronological index, along with links to the more recent columns, appears at www.michbar.org/generalinfo/plainenglish/columns.cfm.

4. U.S.: Rudolf Flesch's Works and Readability Formulas

In the 1930s, researchers began to develop a method of matching the readability (reading ease) of a text with the literacy (reading skill) of adult readers. Early studies showed that certain variables, such as the length of words and sentences, could reliably predict the readability of a text — the level of reading skill required to read and understand it successfully.[6]

In 1943, Rudolf Flesch published his Ph.D. dissertation at Columbia University, *Marks of a Readable Style*.[7] Then in 1948, Flesch published his so-called Reading Ease formula.[8] It graded readability on a scale of 0 to 100, with 0 being very difficult and 100 very easy. The formula uses only two variables: the number of syllables and the number of sentences for each 100-word sample. It became the most widely used of today's popular readability formulas. Regulations in dozens of states require a Reading Ease score of at least 40 in insurance

---

[6] *See, e.g.*, Edgar Dale & Ralph W. Tyler, *A Study of the Factors Influencing the Difficulty of Reading Materials for Adults of Limited Reading Ability*, 4 Library Quarterly 384 (1934), summarized and reprinted in William H. DuBay, *Unlocking Language: The Classic Readability Studies* 78 (Impact Information 2007).

[7] Columbia University Contributions to Education, No. 897 (Teachers College, Columbia University).

[8] Rudolf Flesch, *A New Readability Yardstick*, 32 J. Applied Psychology 221 (1948), summarized and reprinted in DuBay, *supra* n. 6, at 222.

contracts.[9] A modified version of the formula, called the Flesch–Kincaid Grade Level, relies on average sentence length and the average number of syllables per word. Computerized versions of both formulas are available online and on word-processing programs.

Flesch published dozens of popular books on readability, including *The Art of Plain Talk* (1946), *Why Johnny Can't Read* (1955), *The Art of Readable Writing* (2d ed. 1974), and *How to Write Plain English: A Book for Lawyers and Consumers* (1979).

There are other readability formulas. Two of the more reliable are the SMOG formula, by Harry McLaughlin, and the Fog Index, by Robert Gunning. Another is the Dale–Chall formula, published by Edgar Dale and Jeanne Chall in 1948 and updated in 1995.[10] Unlike most other formulas that use word length as a measure of difficulty, it uses a list of 3,000 fourth-grade-level words.

In applying the readability formulas, it's important to remember all the things they don't do. They don't measure purpose, emphasis, organization, coherence, rhetoric, tone, design, or the other factors of effective writing. What they do well is predict the difficulty of a text, since the word-and-sentence factors used in the formulas are among the first causes of reading difficulty. Yet paying attention to those factors alone does not guarantee a clear and readable text.

There are over a thousand studies on readability. For a brief introduction to that research, see the online paper *The Principles of Readability*, by William H. DuBay.[11] The details about each formula mentioned above and calculators are also

---

[9] For a list, see Joseph Kimble, *Plain English: A Charter for Clear Writing*, 9 Thomas M. Cooley L. Rev. 1, 32–35 (1992).

[10] Jeanne S. Chall & Edgar Dale, *Readability Revisited: The New Dale–Chall Readability Formula* (Brookline Books 1995).

[11] http://www.nald.ca/library/research/readab/readab.pdf.

available online.[12] The calculators may give somewhat different numbers (even for the same formula), so consider an average of the formulas or at least compare them against each other.

5. UK: Ernest Gowers's Book *The Complete Plain Words*

Ernest Gowers ran London's civil defense through the Second World War. In a talk to his workers on civil-service English, he said officials tended to be obscure, verbose, and pompous, "using words to cloak their meaning rather than convey it."[13] The talk was so well received that he was asked to write a training pamphlet for civil-service workers. That was the modest start of something big.

Before long, the pamphlet had developed into a book, *Plain Words*, published by His Majesty's Stationery Office in 1948. Within 18 months, 200,000 copies were sold, reaching a far broader readership than was originally envisioned.

> When *Plain Words* first came out, in April 1948, it was evident to those with an ear for such things that here was something quite outstanding in the art of writing lucid prose. . . . For many of us the war . . . had involved a running fight with the flood of turgid circulars descending ceaselessly from above. It seemed almost too good to be true when Sir Ernest produced these lessons for officialdom, and the wonder grew when his little book ran into seven printings before the year was out.[14]

---

[12] http://www.readabilityformulas.com (free); http://www.micropower andlight.com (charges a fee); *see also* http://www.stylewriter-usa.com (offers plain-English editing software, with a Bog Index).

[13] *Official English: Talk by Sir Ernest Gowers to London Region Social Club* 2–3 (Feb. 10, 1943) (issued as a pamphlet).

[14] *The Tablet* (Apr. 23, 1966) (as quoted in Ann Scott, *Ernest Gowers: Plain Words and Forgotten Deeds* 176 (Palgrave Macmillan 2009)).

In 1951, Gowers published a companion text, *The ABC of Plain Words* — an alphabetical reference book "to be kept on the desk and consulted on points of difficulty as they arise."[15] The two books were combined into *The Complete Plain Words* in 1954.[16] That book has since been reprinted many times. It was revised twice: first in 1973 by Sir Bruce Fraser, and then in 1986 by Sidney Greenbaum and Janet Whitcut. In both instances, the revisers affirmed its "deep and lasting influence" in the public service.[17] They might have added "as well as the public at large."

6. UK: Renton Committee Report on Legislation

In May 1973, a Committee on the Preparation of Legislation was established by the UK government under the chairmanship of Sir David (later, Lord) Renton. Its terms of reference were to review the form of drafting in public bills "with a view to achieving greater simplicity and clarity in statute law."[18]

The Committee published its report, called *The Preparation of Legislation*, in May 1975. Chapter 6 detailed the many criticisms about obscurity in UK statute law, and among the report's 121 recommendations were the following (mostly in chapter 11):

- Use purpose clauses to clarify the scope and effect of legislation.

---

[15] *The ABC of Plain Words* iii (HM Stationery Off. 1951).

[16] *The Complete Plain Words* (HM Stationery Off. 1954).

[17] *Id.* at iii (rev. ed., HM Stationery Off. 1973) and at xxiii (rev. U.S. ed., David R. Godine 1988). A third revision, by Gowers's great-granddaughter Rebecca Gowers, is due from Penguin Books in 2013.

[18] Committee Appointed by the Lord President of the Council, *The Preparation of Legislation* iii (May 1975).

- Limit the body of a statute to general principles and relegate details to schedules and delegated legislation.
- Arrange statutes to suit the users' convenience.
- Make greater use both of examples showing how a bill is intended to work in particular situations and of simple mathematical formulas.
- Avoid long, unparagraphed sentences.
- Avoid cross-referring definitions.
- Explore methods for highlighting defined terms.
- Use larger type for schedules.
- End the practice of enacting a law that changes the substance of an existing law without actually changing its text.

Unfortunately, the report is not now easily accessible. But when Lord Renton died in May 2007, his obituary in the *Daily Telegraph* paid tribute to the report:

> [Its] proposals ran into powerful opposition behind the scenes from the parliamentary legal establishment, and the government quietly abandoned them. Nonetheless, it remains the seminal work on the subject.[19]

7. Australia: Michèle Asprey's Book *Plain Language for Lawyers*

In 1990, before Asprey wrote *Plain Language for Lawyers*, there were few legal texts explaining how lawyers could write legal documents in plain language and why they should.

---

[19] http://www.telegraph.co.uk/news/obituaries/1552525/Lord-Renton.html; *see also* Lord Simon of Glaisdale, *The Renton Report — Ten Years On*, 6 Statute L. Rev. 133, 134 (1985) (describing the report as having a "fundamental positive significance" because it is a "first-rate state paper against which legislative shortcomings can be measured and to whose authority appeal may be made").

Certainly, this book was the first in Australia to do that, and right away universities and law schools across Australia took it up.

Before she wrote the book, Asprey was a commercial lawyer with one of Australia's largest law firms and then director of legal precedents (forms) at another large firm. That experience is reflected in the book: while it takes a practical point of view and is highly readable, it also shows Asprey's years of research into legal language and has all the references and footnotes that a lawyer could wish for. *Plain Language for Lawyers* stands out as the single most comprehensive book on the subject. It covers all the bases. And one of its chapters, detailing international developments in plain language, is now available as a stand-alone e-book.[20]

The fourth edition was published in 2010 — almost 20 years after the first. The book has had a powerful influence not just in Australia but also in Europe, in the Americas, and throughout Asia. There's even a special edition for India.

LAWS AND RULES

8. U.S.: New York's Plain-English Law — and Other State Statutes That Followed

Within a month of the press conference to announce the Citibank loan note (see highlight 14), a New York assemblyman began working on a bill to require plain English in every contract between a consumer and business in the state. It was passed in 1977 and amended in 1978.[21] And in the years that followed, at least ten other states adopted statutes that,

---

[20] http://digital.federationpress.com.au/14r2jh.
[21] N.Y. Gen. Oblig. Law § 5-702 (McKinney 2001 (latest published set)).

in one way or another, require plain English in consumer contracts generally.[22]

The salutary effect of these laws has belied the original concern about waves of litigation. In New York, for instance, the law produced fewer than ten lawsuits in its first 30 years.[23] What's more:

> [B]usinesses [in New York] reacted to the new law by rewriting their forms in language that makes more sense to the non-lawyer. Whether all forms are as simple as they might be is in some doubt. What is not in doubt, however, is that [Peter] Sullivan's Plain English law has indeed achieved the climate he sought.[24]

The same goes for New Jersey, where the regulatory officer who reviewed contracts for compliance said in 1997 that the New Jersey law "has proved to be extremely effective," that "individual businesses have cooperated fully," and that "no disruptions . . . arose . . . because of the new consumer-contract standards."[25] After 14 years, there had been exactly four lawsuits over noncompliance in New Jersey — and none

---

[22] Conn. Gen. Stat. Ann. §§ 42-151 to 42-158 (West 2007); Haw. Rev. Stat. Ann. §§ 487A-1 to 487A-4 (Lexis 2009); 10 Me. Rev. Stat. Ann. §§ 1121–1126 (2009); Minn. Stat. Ann. §§ 325G.29 to 325G.37 (West 2011); Mont. Code Ann. §§ 30-14-1101 to 30-14-1104, 30-14-1111 to 30-14-1113 (2011); N.J. Stat. Ann. §§ 56:12-1 to 56:12-13 (West 2001); Or. Rev. Stat. Ann. §§ 180.540 to 180.555 (West 2007 & Supp. 2011); Pa. Stat. Ann. title 73, §§ 2201–2212 (West 2008); Tex. Fin. Code Ann. § 341.502 (Vernon 2006 & Supp. 2011); W. Va. Code Ann. § 46A-6-109 (Lexis 2006).

[23] Duncan MacDonald, *The Story of a Famous Promissory Note*, 10 Scribes J. Legal Writing 79, 88 (2005–2006).

[24] Carl Felsenfeld, *The Future of Plain English*, 62 Mich. B.J. 942, 942–43 (Nov. 1983) (footnote omitted); *see also* Rosemary Moukad, *New York's Plain English Law*, 8 Fordham Urban L.J. 451, 462 (1979) (reporting on a survey of more than 200 organizations, 75% of which had revised or were revising their documents).

[25] Kimble, *Don't Stop Now: An Open Letter to the SEC*, in *Lifting the Fog of Legalese*, *supra* n. 1, at 49, 51–52.

in Minnesota after 14 years.[26] No other state has reported a different experience.

9. U.S.: Securities and Exchange Commission's Plain-English Rules and *Plain English Handbook*

Plain language got its start at the SEC in the mid-1990s through the leadership of Chairman Arthur Levitt. He knew that for investors to enjoy the fundamental protections provided by securities laws, they needed investment documents they could easily read and understand. He created an Office of Investor Education, whose director, Nancy Smith, worked with Ann Wallace in the Division of Corporation Finance on a unique approach to promoting plain language.

Rather than starting with a proposed administrative rule, Smith and Wallace sought corporate volunteers willing to file disclosure documents in plain English in return for a shorter review period of the filings. Bell Atlantic and NYNEX, which were planning to merge, quickly stepped forward, and in September 1996 they mailed to stockholders what was probably the first plain-English joint proxy statement.[27] Although the companies were concerned about possible liability, they discovered that "[i]n many ways we reduced our liability because we . . . created a document that [was] much clearer and less ambiguous."[28] Eventually, over 75 public companies filed documents in plain English during the pilot project.

---

[26] *Id.* at 52.

[27] George Hathaway & Kathleen Gibson, *The Word from the Securities and Exchange Commission: Put It in Plain English*, 75 Mich. B.J. 1314, 1314 (Dec. 1996) (containing several before-and-after examples).

[28] *Id.*

Also during the project, the SEC, with help from experts William Lutz, Ken Morris, and Alan Siegel, drafted the superb *Plain English Handbook*, which is still available on the SEC website.[29]

Then in 1998, with the groundwork firmly laid, the SEC adopted its plain-English rules. One rule sets out plain-English principles for the front and back covers, any summary, and any risk-factor section of a prospectus.[30] The other rule sets out guidance for the requirement that the rest of a prospectus be "clear, concise, and understandable."[31] Although many earlier federal statutes and regulations had required "clear" or "understandable" language, the SEC rules were the first to try to state that requirement more specifically.[32]

10. U.S.: Plain Writing Act of 2010

In 2006, the Center for Plain Language (see highlight 27) began a campaign to educate Congress about the need for a federal law — no less — requiring the government to write clearly to citizens. Those efforts, led by Annetta Cheek, paid off in early 2007, when Representative Bruce Braley of Iowa introduced a plain-language act in the U.S. House. Early in 2008, Daniel Akaka of Hawaii introduced a companion law in the U.S. Senate. While the act passed the House by a healthy margin — 376 to 1 — it failed to reach the Senate floor because Robert Bennett of Utah placed a hold on it. So the 110th Congress closed with no plain-language act in place.

---

[29] http://www.sec.gov/pdf/handbook.pdf.

[30] 17 C.F.R. § 230.421(d) (2011).

[31] *Id.* § 230.421(b).

[32] *See* Thomas M. Clyde, *Plain Language Turns the Corner: New SEC Rules for Prospectuses*, 42 Clarity 9 (Sept. 1998) (discussing the rules' specific requirements).

Early in the 111th Congress (which started in January 2009), both sponsors from the previous Congress reintroduced their bills. Again the House version passed, 386 to 33, and again the Senate version was held by Bennett. But after his party did not renominate him and some changes were made to the bill, he released his hold. Once the bill came to the Senate floor, it passed unanimously.[33]

The Plain Writing Act defines "plain writing" to mean writing that is clear, concise, and well-organized, and that follows other best practices appropriate to the subject or field and intended audience. It covers both paper and electronic information. Although it does not apply to federal regulations (there were political obstacles), it applies to any other document that:

(1) is necessary for obtaining any federal-government benefit or service or for filing taxes;

(2) provides information about any federal-government benefit or service; or

(3) explains to the public how to comply with a requirement that the federal government administers or enforces.

To achieve its purpose, the Act sets out a series of steps that each agency must take. It also requires the Office of Management and Budget to develop and issue guidance on implementing the Act. The Office designated the U.S. federal PLAIN group (see highlight 26) as the interagency working group to help with guidance. And that guidance was issued in April 2011.[34]

---

[33] Pub. L. No. 111-274, 124 Stat. 2861 (2010) (available at http://www.gpo.gov/fdsys/pkg/PLAW-111publ274/pdf/PLAW-111publ274.pdf).

[34] Memo. from Cass R. Sunstein, Administrator, Office of Information & Regulatory Affairs, to Heads of Executive Dep'ts & Agencies, *Final Guidance on Implementing the Plain Writing Act of 2010* (Apr. 13, 2011) (available at http://www.whitehouse.gov/sites/default/files/omb/memoranda/2011/m11-15.pdf).

For more about the Act and its history, see Annetta L. Cheek, *The Plain Writing Act of 2010: Getting Democracy to Work for You*, 90 Mich. B.J. 52 (Oct. 2011).

11. European Union: Unfair Contract Terms Directive

Since 1993, consumers in European Union member states have benefited from a law — EC Council Directive 93/13[35] — requiring standard-form consumer contracts to be in plain language. Article 2 does not define that term but simply provides:

> In the case of contracts where all or certain terms offered to the consumer are in writing, these terms must always be drafted in plain, intelligible language. Where there is doubt about the meaning of a term, the interpretation most favourable to the consumer shall prevail.

Article 3.1 addresses unfairness:

> A contractual term which has not been individually negotiated shall be regarded as unfair if, contrary to the requirement of good faith, it causes a significant imbalance in the parties' rights and obligations under the contract, to the detriment of the consumer.

The European law arose after pressure from consumer bodies, including the EU-wide European Consumers' Organization.

As the law itself requires, EU member states have since transposed it into their own national legislation, such as the UK's Unfair Terms in Consumer Contracts Regulation 1999 (replacing a 1994 version).[36] The resulting improvements have

---

[35] Available at http://eur-lex.europa.eu/LexUriServ/LexUriServ.do?uri=OJ:L:1993:095:0029:0034:EN:PDF.

[36] Available at http://www.legislation.gov.uk/uksi/1999/2083/pdfs/uksi_19992083_en.pdf.

been striking, with many companies sweeping away small print and the worst legalese as they seek to comply.

The main legal enforcers in the UK are the Office of Fair Trading and the Financial Services Authority, which regularly outlaw companies' use of words like *indemnify* and *indemnity* because consumers are unlikely to know what they mean or to understand their significance. The Office has issued its Unfair Contract Terms Guidance.[37] Besides providing guidance on unfair terms in various kinds of contracts, it addresses unfair standard terms — and notes:

> Regulation 7 [of the 1999 UK regulations] requires that plain and intelligible language is used in consumer contracts. A term is open to challenge as unfair if it could put the consumer at a disadvantage because he or she is not clear about its meaning — even if its meaning could be worked out by a lawyer.[38]

There you go: people should not need a lawyer to "work out" most consumer contracts. The EU has it right. And if the UK is any indication, the 1993 Directive has prompted significant change.

12. South Africa: Constitution

The South African Constitution, which took effect in 1997, is the product of a deeply democratic process. Its principles were developed through negotiations among all parties before South Africa's first democratic elections. Much of its detailed content was generated from widespread public participation, the results of which were synthesized by a

---

[37] Office of Fair Trading, *Unfair Contract Terms Guidance* (Sept. 2008) (available at http://www.oft.gov.uk/shared_oft/reports/unfair_contract_terms/oft311.pdf).

[38] Office of Fair Trading, *Unfair Standard Terms* 3 (Sept. 2008) (available at http://www.oft.gov.uk/shared_oft/business_leaflets/unfair_contract_terms/oft143.pdf).

Constitutional Committee made up of representatives from the political parties elected in 1994. It was passed by a Constitutional Assembly made up of both houses of the democratically elected Parliament. And it is written in a language that speaks for and to everyone.[39]

The Constitutional Committee required the legislative drafters to apply principles of plain language in drafting the Constitution. Those principles are reflected in its organization, sentence structure, and vocabulary.

The Preamble uses four bullet points to eloquently set out the Constitution's purpose, one of which is to "[h]eal the divisions of the past and establish a society based on democratic values, social justice, and fundamental human rights." The chapters that follow are arranged to begin with the most important provisions — the foundational principles of the Republic in chapter 1, and the Bill of Rights in chapter 2. The first right, as one would expect in a society with such a long and intense history of inequality, is the right to equality: "Everyone is equal before the law and has the right to equal protection and benefit of the law." The rights then cascade down through a comprehensive and stirring series, from civil rights ("Everyone has inherent dignity") and political rights ("Everyone has the right to vote") to social and economic rights ("Everyone has the right to a basic education"). After that, in a logical sequence, come the chapters on the divisions and processes of government.

The language throughout is plain. Some may (incorrectly) consider it simplistic. In fact, to draft in this way requires a huge dedication of resources, highly skilled and dedicated drafters, and a firm commitment to the goal of clarity.[40] Plain

---

[39] Available at http://www.info.gov.za/documents/constitution.

[40] *See* Peg James, *Drafters of South Africa's New Constitution Adapt to Plain Language*, 38 Clarity 13, 15 (Jan. 1997) (reporting on a survey in which the drafters' "most frequent response was that plain language increased clarity").

language done well is extremely hard work, yet worth it. For 15 years, the courts have had little difficulty interpreting and applying the Constitution — a testimony to both its clarity and its legal rigor. The Constitution has been effective as a social, political, and legal text. And at the same time, it can be understood by the citizens of the new country it formed.

13. South Africa: Consumer Protection Act

In his opening address at a 1995 seminar called "Plain Language, the Law and the Right to Information," the then Minister of Justice in South Africa, Mr. Dullah Omar, spoke about the transformation of justice. Not long before that, the country had held its first democratic elections. Minister Omar outlined several key principles as being important to achieve transformation in South Africa: the principles of access to justice, participation, and empowerment. He believed that plain language was a fundamental right for citizens — "an absolute and critical necessity for democracy" — and called for it in the country's laws, in government and business communications, on TV, and on the radio.[41]

Since then, several laws have been passed in South Africa to redress the imbalances of the apartheid era. After the Constitution, the most notable of these laws is the Consumer Protection Act (No. 68 of 2008),[42] which took effect in March 2011.

Among many other provisions to protect consumers, the Act requires that information be given in plain language. This is stated as a fundamental right — just as the Minister of Justice had described it — and the requirement may not be

---

[41] Dullah Omar, *Plain Language, the Law and the Right to Information*, 33 Clarity 11, 13–14 (July 1995).

[42] Available at http://www.info.gov.za/view/DownloadFileAction? id=99961.

circumvented by contract. Section 22(2) gives a detailed definition of plain language:

> For the purposes of this Act, a notice, document or visual representation is in plain language if it is reasonable to conclude that an ordinary consumer of the class of persons for whom the notice, document or visual representation is intended, with average literacy skills and minimal experience as a consumer of the relevant goods or services, could be expected to understand the content, significance and import of the notice, document or visual representation without undue effort, having regard to —
>
> (a) the context, comprehensiveness and consistency of the notice, document or visual representation;
> (b) the organization, form and style of the notice, document or visual representation;
> (c) the vocabulary, usage and sentence structure of the notice, document or visual representation; and
> (d) the use of any illustrations, examples, headings or other aids to reading and understanding.

The Act applies not only to businesses but to the government as well. The penalty for not complying is R1 million or 10% of a business's net turnover, whichever is the greater (Section 112(2)). So businesses have been scrambling to comply. (Most cellphone companies, for instance, have received notices requiring them to explain various contract terms.) But the government has been slower to comply, and it remains to be seen whether the Act will have the full bite it promises.

PROJECTS AND ACTIVITIES

14. U.S.: Citibank's Loan Note

In 1975, Citibank fired the simplification shot heard around the world — or at least around the United States. The '70s were of course the heyday of the consumer movement, which partly drove the Citibank project.

The primary authors of the simplified loan note were Duncan MacDonald, Alan Siegel, and Carl Felsenfeld. The old note ran about 3,000 words; the revised note was about 600 words. So the old one obviously contained a mass of unnecessary content and detail. What's more, both notes fit onto a single sheet of 8½-by-14-inch paper, so the print in the original was almost microscopic and, just as bad, mostly in all-capital letters. Naturally, the bank's law firm objected to the new note as "reckless" — "it scared the daylights out of the lawyers."[43] After Citibank held a press conference to announce it, the note made a big splash in the local media and "on front pages across the United States."[44]

For a lively behind-the-scenes account of the Citibank note, see the article cited in footnote 23. For the before-and-after versions of the note, see Peter M. Tiersma, *Legal Language* appendix E (U. Chicago Press 1999).

15. U.S.: Redrafting of Federal Court Rules

Four sets of rules govern the procedure in all the 94 U.S. federal district courts and the 13 courts of appeals. And in a process that took 20 years, those four sets were completely

---

[43] MacDonald, *supra* n. 23, at 81, 82.

[44] *Id.* at 85.

redrafted — or "restyled" — for clarity, consistency, and plain language.

In the early 1990s, the Standing Committee on Federal Rules decided to face up to the deficiencies caused by many years of not taking a systematic, expert approach to drafting. The Standing Committee appointed a style subcommittee, whose first drafting consultant was Bryan Garner. In 1996, the Administrative Office of the United States published his *Guidelines for Drafting and Editing Court Rules*,[45] which has indeed guided all four restyling projects. The Rules of Appellate Procedure were approved in 1998; the Rules of Criminal Procedure in 2002; the Rules of Civil Procedure in 2007; and the Rules of Evidence in 2011. Garner was the drafting consultant for the first two sets, and I was for the last two. But each project of course involved intensive work over several years by a committee of judges, lawyers, and professors.

Although there was some opposition along the way, the revisions accomplished their goal. The new rules are a striking improvement.[46] They have won two Burton Awards for Reform in Law and a ClearMark Award from the Center for Plain Language. To date, there has not been a flood of lawsuits claiming that the rules created inadvertent substantive changes. In a very few instances, unintended changes were quickly fixed, as any others will be if the appropriate committees see the need. In short, "each of the restyling projects

---

[45] Available at http://www.uscourts.gov/uscourts/RulesAndPolicies/rules/guide.pdf.

[46] *See* Joseph Kimble, *Lessons in Drafting from the New Federal Rules of Civil Procedure*, 12 Scribes J. Legal Writing 25 (2008–2009) (available at http://www.uscourts.gov/uscourts/RulesAndPolicies/rules/Style%20Resources/Lessons%20in%20Drafting.pdf) (containing 50 pages of examples).

has proved enormously successful."[47] And now some states have started to redraft their court rules — which tend to follow the federal rules — in the same plain style.

16. Canada: Reports on Access to the Law and Events That Followed

In Canada, plain language has been strongly — and rightly — influenced by the idea that the public should have access to the law.

As long ago as 1975, a report by Martin Friedland for the Law Reform Commission of Canada confirmed the public's difficulty in finding and understanding legal information. The report, called *Access to the Law*, is somewhat hard to find, but a summary is available online.[48] Researchers asked almost 200 Canadian citizens ten law-related questions that they might face in daily life. The citizens sought answers from a variety of sources, and the researchers then checked with those sources. The researchers found that more than 25% of the sources gave an incorrect answer. As one of several solutions, the report suggested that statutes can be improved by "using more readable language; improving [their] sentence structure; including comments and examples after each section; using formulas, graphs, and charts, where applicable; . . . putting definitions in bold throughout the statute . . . ; [and] using [an] explanatory memorandum to explain the statute and its purpose."[49] Quite enlightened for the time.

---

[47] Memo. from Robert Hinkle, Chair, *Report of the Advisory Committee on Evidence Rules* 3 (May 10, 2010) (available at http://www.uscourts.gov/uscourts/RulesAndPolicies/rules/jc09-2010/2010-09-Appendix-D.pdf).

[48] http://www.legalresearchandwriting.ca/images/TEDTJADEN-Chapter6.pdf.

[49] *Id.* at 205.

Then, in 1988, came a report called *Access to Justice* by the Justice Reform Committee of British Columbia. Chapter 6 of that report was devoted to plain language.[50] The chapter outlined the plain-language movement in Canada and elsewhere and concluded that the attorney general in British Columbia should establish a plain-language committee to develop a strategy for introducing plain language into the justice system.

Although the effects of these two reports are difficult to specifically trace, it's likely that they rippled throughout the federal and provincial governments:

- In 1989, the Department of Multiculturalism and Citizenship Canada conducted three-day training sessions across the country. And in 1991, the Department published a manual called *Plain Language: Clear and Simple*, written in English and French. It was in print for 20 years.

- In 1990, the Canadian Bar Association and Canadian Bankers Association published a report called *The Decline and Fall of Gobbledygook*, recommending ways to promote plain language in the legal profession and in banking.

- In 1991, the Canadian Bar Association adopted the recommendations contained in the report.

- In 1990, the attorney general of British Columbia established the Plain Language Institute of British Columbia, which produced a body of research and publications in the 1990s.

- From 1990 to 1993, the Continuing Legal Education Society of British Columbia made a concerted effort to train lawyers in plain language and to convert their forms into plain language.

---

[50] Chapter 6 is available from the author.

- In 1990, Alberta passed a Financial Consumers Act requiring "readily understandable language and form" in financial products.[51] It was Canada's first plain-language statute.
- In 1992, the Alberta Law Reform Institute published several model plain-language documents — and the Institute is still doing good work (see highlight 30).

17. Canada: Training in Provincial Securities Commissions and the Rewriting of Investment-Industry Rules

Canada is the only country in the G20 without a national securities regulator. But over the past decade, the attention paid to plain language in provincial securities commissions has been remarkable.

To kick off the new millennium, the British Columbia Securities Commission started training sessions that even included its chair, Doug Hyndman. The first year, all 220 staff members attended a two-day plain-writing workshop, with materials tailored from their own documents. The training was conducted by Wordsmith Associates Communications Consultants.

Over the decade, the Commission has done the following:

- Created, and updated in 2008, a *Plain Language Style Guide* for staff — still available to the public through the Commission's website.[52]
- Trained plain-language mentors.
- Conducted annual plain-language audits by collecting samples of cross-organizational writing.

---

[51] Rev. Stat. Alb. 2000, chapter F-13, § 13(1).

[52] http://www.bcsc.bc.ca/uploadedFiles/BCSC_Plain_Language_Style_Guide_2008.pdf.

- Offered refresher programs based on the first audit samples.
- Trained all new employees every year.

The Ontario Securities Commission followed British Columbia's lead and started training from the top. It, too, developed a *Plain Language Style Guide* (available internally but not publicly). Over the years, Wordsmith also conducted workshops for securities commissions in Alberta, Manitoba, Québec, and New Brunswick.

In 2007, the national Investment Dealers Association began to sponsor training sessions for its legal and other staff in cities throughout Canada. Then in 2008, the Association merged into the Investment Industry Regulatory Organization of Canada, a national self-regulatory organization that oversees investment dealers and trading organizations and reports to the provincial securities commissions. It has spent several years rewriting its dealer-member rules in plain language.[53] They have not been completely rewritten in a century.

18. UK: Government-Wide Review of Forms

Margaret Thatcher became the British Prime Minister in May 1979 and brought in private-sector expertise to overhaul what she saw as a bloated government bureaucracy that stifled business enterprise. Sir Derek Rayner, on temporary leave from a directorship at Marks & Spencer, headed a team of civil-service high-flyers who had the power to persuade departments to change their ways. Sir Derek saw better, clearer forms as a good thing because they would save time

---

[53] *See New IIROC Rule Book* (May 2009) (available at http://www.iiroc.ca/English/Policy/IIROCRuleBook/Documents/IIROCRuleBookSummaryStatusReport_en.pdf) (setting out the goals and process).

and money. What's more, he'd then be able to understand them himself, he reportedly said.

The main outcome of the Rayner review came in March 1982 when the government issued a White Paper, *Administrative Forms in Government*. The considerable good work that followed is described in part 5 (see summary 9).

19. UK: Tax-Law Revision

For 15 years, the UK pursued a project to rewrite its tax legislation. Originally, in 1995, the project had been estimated to take five years. It ended in 2010, having completed the rewriting of income tax and corporation tax. It ended in part through exhaustion.

The seven rewritten Acts[54] have substantially added to the length of tax legislation. This aspect of the rewrite has attracted criticism. The decision to split income tax and corporation tax (which were previously dealt with in the same Act) and rewrite each one separately led to unavoidable repetition. Still, the benefits are clear: legislation that's better organized for a particular taxpayer (even if repeated elsewhere for another), coupled with simpler and more accessible language — especially for younger practitioners not steeped in the older, more archaic style.

And there have been long-term benefits — namely, the general lessons that parliamentary drafters have learned about better structure, shorter sections, the use of formulas and method statements, consistent definitions, the use of signposts and overviews within the Acts, and simpler language. At the very least, then, the project has been an agent for change and for reexamining existing practices.

---

[54] Capital Allowances Act 2001, Income Tax (Earnings and Pensions) Act 2003, Income Tax (Trading and Other Income) Act 2005, Income Tax Act 2007, Corporation Tax Act 2009, Corporation Tax Act 2010, Taxation (International and Other Provisions) Act 2010.

20. Norway: Civil-Service Project

In 2007, partly in reaction to serious complaints from the public about obscurity in some letters dealing with pensions, the Minister of Government Administration, Reform and Church Affairs, Heidi Grande Røys, started a plain-language pilot project. In the next year or so, the Ministry encouraged a few government agencies to improve some of their forms and letters that were intended for large groups. The success of that effort led the Ministry to broaden the requirements to include the government's entire civil service.

The expanded project, called Plain Language in Norway's Civil Service, started in 2008 and was originally intended to end in 2010. The project was led by the Agency for Public Management and e-Government, in close cooperation with the Language Council of Norway (see highlight 35). The goal was "to promote clearer language and more accessible content in public documents and publications intended for citizens."[55] As the project was about to end, the Ministry decided to extend it for another two years, until December 31, 2012. One of the main priorities will be improving the language in laws and regulations.

Among the project's achievements in the first two years:

- www.klarsprak.no. This website includes advice, tools, and tips on how written language can be made more user-friendly, clear, and understandable, and how to successfully carry out plain-language projects. The resources on the website are open for anyone to use, and agencies are encouraged to share their experiences and results.

- Lectures and training courses. The project team arranges lectures, seminars, and conferences for agencies

---

[55] As described at http://sprakradet.no/nb-NO/Klarsprak/Diverse/Toppmeny5/In-English.

and other interested organizations. And civil servants can attend courses on writing clearly.

• Project grants and support. Government agencies can apply for funding for programs and get advice from plain-language experts.

• A plain-language award. An annual award goes to a government agency that has made an extraordinary effort to improve the clarity of its written information for the public.

• A project guide. It gives advice on how to run a plain-language project. Selected government agencies and local municipalities describe what they have achieved so far and the lessons learned.

An evaluation of the project and the agencies' work is in progress. It will be completed in 2013 — and promises to be the first of its kind. The results will benefit future plain-language work not only in Norway but in other countries as well. Every project adds a chapter to the plain-language story.

21. Australia: NRMA's Car-Insurance Policy

In early 1976, the National Roads and Motorists' Association Insurance Company issued its car-insurance policy for the first time in plain language. A first for an Australian legal document, a first for the country.

Of course, lawyers were skeptical and boasted that they'd capitalize on the new policy. But the company was determined that its customers should be able to understand their rights and responsibilities. And with the help of Robert Eagleson, an early leader in plain language, the company succeeded admirably.

Perhaps the most surprising initial benefit was a wave of good publicity. Everybody seemed to be reading about the policy and commenting on it. Later, the company itself identified a number of more tangible benefits: a reduction in the number of invalid claims, since customers could better understand their coverage; less time to train staff and more efficiency in handling claims; and an actual reduction in lawsuits over wording in the policy.[56] The lawyers' expectations were dashed.

What's even more, the policy became a stimulus to other efforts. Within a year, the Real Estate Institute of New South Wales had recast its standard residential and commercial leases.[57] Within seven years, the Australian government had launched a plain-language policy within its departments.[58] And within ten years, the Law Reform Commission of Victoria (see highlight 37) had shown that legislation — traditionally a stronghold of legalese — could find surer expression in plain language. Now most parliamentary drafting offices in Australia have embraced plain language, as have several major law firms (see highlight 22). Legalese has been knocked off its pedestal in Australia.

22. Australia: Progress in Major Law Firms

Once the Australian legal profession stopped opposing plain language, law-firm clients began demanding clearer letters of advice and clearer contracts. In response, the profession has moved steadily — though sometimes slowly, and always carefully — toward a plainer style.

The first developments were in the mid-1990s, when several people involved in the Law Reform Commission of Victoria's plain-language work (see highlight 37) moved on to become practitioners. Professor Robert Eagleson joined

---

[56] Neville King, *An Experience with Plain English*, 61 Current Affairs Bulletin 21, 21 (Jan. 1985).

[57] Robert Eagleson, *The Commonsense of Plain English*, 61 Current Affairs Bulletin 14, 14 (Jan. 1985).

[58] *Id.* at 14–15.

the major commercial firm Mallesons Stephen Jaques as a plain-language consultant, working with Michèle Asprey.[59] Professor David St L Kelly, who had been chair of the Commission, and Christopher Balmford, who worked there in a rewriting role, joined the leading insurance firm Phillips Fox. Also, Judith Bennett, who had worked at the Centre for Plain Legal Language (see highlight 38), joined the major commercial firm Freehills.

In each firm, these advocates-turned-practitioners rewrote documents for clients; revised forms; trained lawyers throughout the firm; and continued to advocate for plain language, both within their firms and elsewhere. Gradually, other firms joined in the move to a clearer writing style. Competition took effect.

Over the years, most major Australian law firms have:

- Arranged plain-language training for many of their lawyers.

- Revamped their document-design standards to increase the use of headings, reduce the allowed levels of hierarchy, and otherwise make their documents visually more appealing and easier to read.

- Rewritten forms and prepared dramatically different models for their letters of advice.

The law firms' interest in plain language has naturally spread to lawyers working in government departments, non-profits, and commercial organizations.

To be sure, lawyers still have a way to go, and many who claim to write in plain language actually write quite poorly. But Australia can probably claim a higher conversion rate and greater public commitment among major firms than any other country.

---

[59] Edward Kerr, *Using Plain Language in Law Firms*, 73 Mich. B.J. 48 (Jan. 1994).

23. Australia: Format of Legislation

Australia was the first English-speaking country to apply the principles of clear design to legislation. In the early 1990s, two important reports were published: *Access to the Law: The Structure and Format of Legislation*[60] and *Clearer Commonwealth Law.*[61] The first of these two publications was especially influential and offered striking examples of how legislation could be made easier to use.

But it was through a joint project between the New South Wales Parliamentary Counsel's Office and the Centre for Plain Legal Language (see highlight 38) that the ideas for better design were first officially carried out. The project began in 1991 and included a survey of users to confirm the difficulties they had with the existing design. The review team came up with better designs and tested them to make sure that readers found them easier to use. The results were published in a 1994 discussion paper, *Review and Redesign of NSW Legislation*. Among the recommended new features:

- Running headers that include part, division, and section number, as well as the part name — to show readers exactly where they are in the statute.
- Headings that use a distinctive sans-serif font to make them stand out from the text, and graduated sizes to show their hierarchy.
- Headings set flush left, with all text slightly indented, for easy scanning.
- More white space between sections.
- Hanging indents for all vertical lists.

---

[60] Law Reform Comm'n of Victoria, Report No. 33 (1990).
[61] House of Representatives Standing Committee on Legal & Constitutional Affairs (Sept. 1993) (including a chapter on "Presentation of Legislation").

The important thing is that these design features were actually adopted by the New South Wales attorney general. Beginning in 1995, all legislation followed the new format.[62] Thus, New South Wales was the first jurisdiction in the common-law world to make such dramatic changes to legislative design. Because the design was easier to navigate, it also helped the move toward publishing legislation electronically (although some design features may be altered in the process).

Other jurisdictions across Australia soon followed suit. In the federal government, for instance, parliamentary drafters have taken the enlightened step of using examples, tables, and diagrams in legislation.[63] And in 2000, New Zealand adopted formatting changes similar to Australia's.[64]

24. New Zealand: WriteMark and Plain English Power

In 2000, tired of claims by commercial and government organizations that they wrote in plain language when their documents showed otherwise, plain-language consultant Lynda Harris saw the need for a writing standard. After much research and testing, she launched a plain-English quality mark, the WriteMark, in 2005. The WriteMark is a techniques-based assessment that also encourages user-testing.

---

[62] *See, e.g.*, Evidence Act 1995 No. 25 (available at http://www.legislation. nsw.gov.au/sessionalview/sessional/act/1995-25.pdf).

[63] *See* Office of Parliamentary Counsel, *Working with the OPC — A Guide for Clients*, part H, 57–61 (available at http://www.opc.gov.au/about/ docs/Working_With_OPC.pdf) (demonstrating the use of all three graphic techniques).

[64] For examples, see http://www.pco.parliament.govt.nz/online-legislation.

In 2006, two communications companies, WriteMark and Write Group, founded the nonprofit Plain English Awards[65] to expand the WriteMark standards into an awards program for good and bad public documents. The awards program has had a significant influence. For example, in 2006 the Ministry of Social Development received a Brainstrain Award for its bewildering student-loan agreement. The Ministry's chief executive accepted the award, admitted that the agreement was poorly written, and vowed to have it fixed. The loan agreement has since been rewritten in plain English, to the benefit of everyone who takes out a student loan. And there have been other tangible results.[66] The awards are now run by a charitable trust formed specifically to foster a demand for plain English in New Zealand business and government.

Building on the success of the WriteMark standards and awards program, in 2008 a group of plain-language consultants formed a grassroots network of residents and consumer groups called Plain English Power.[67] Plain English Power is lobbying to make plain language a permanent, government-wide legal requirement, comparable to the U.S. Plain Writing Act of 2010 (see highlight 10).

---

[65] *See* http://www.plainenglishawards.org.nz.

[66] *See* http://www.plainenglishawards.org.nz/are-the-awards-making-a-difference-2010/.

[67] *See* http://www.plainenglish.org.nz.

ORGANIZATIONS

25. U.S.: Document Design Center at the American Institutes for Research

The Document Design Center was a home for plain-language work from 1979 to 1997. The Center grew out of a three-year government-funded project in which the American Institutes for Research (a nonprofit research organization) collaborated with Carnegie Mellon University and the private design firm Siegel+Gale. The original three-year project had these goals:

- Gather research from many disciplines to help team members understand why public documents are so difficult both to write and to use.
- Do new research to fill in gaps in what was already known.
- Publish and disseminate this research in ways that were useful to practitioners.
- Help government agencies create plain-language documents that could serve as model documents for others to follow.
- Develop new courses and degrees to train future writers — a goal that was carried out through a graduate-degree program in rhetoric and document design at Carnegie Mellon University in Pittsburgh.

Two books by the original project team — one collecting research and the other setting out guidelines — were especially influential.[68] They "established document design as an interdisciplinary field" and "strongly influenced thousands of people in different fields to improve their documents."[69]

Dr. Janice (Ginny) Redish led the original project and became the first director of the Document Design Center. The associate directors were Dr. Veda Charrow and Dr. Robin Battison.

Most of the Center's early work dealt with legal documents — government regulations, notices, letters, and forms. From that work, Dr. Charrow and a lawyer colleague, Myra Erhardt, wrote *Clear and Effective Legal Writing*, now in its fourth edition and still used in many U.S. law schools. From 1979 to 1989, the Center also published a widely circulated newsletter, *Simply Stated*.

From the beginning, the Center used and promoted a process for plain language based on audience and outcomes. The process begins with understanding the purposes for the document; the audience for it; and where, when, how, and for what the audience will use it (the context of use). The process also includes iterative usability testing — making sure that the guidelines used to design, organize, and write the document allow the readers to easily and quickly find what they need, understand what they find, and act appropriately on that understanding.

In the 1980s, the Center focused more on computer documentation than on legal documents, developing some of the earliest examples of user- and task-oriented manuals

---

[68] *See* Daniel B. Felker et al., *Document Design: A Review of the Relevant Research* (American Institutes for Research 1980); Daniel B. Felker et al., *Guidelines for Document Designers* (American Institutes for Research 1981) (available at http://eric.ed.gov/PDFS/ED221866.pdf). The Document Design Project also published 18 technical reports and several book chapters.

[69] Ginny Redish & Susan Kleimann, *The U.S. Document Design Center: A Retrospective*, 43 Clarity 3, 3 (May 1999).

and online help systems. One example: the manuals for IBM's Profs program, which used icons for the manuals' tabs long before icons were common on the screen.

In 1993, Dr. Susan Kleimann took over as the director. She changed the name to the Information Design Center to reflect the growing interest in online and voice media. The Center continued to work with many federal agencies, and for one, the Veterans Benefits Administration, the Center developed a very successful course on reader-focused writing. More than 10,000 VBA and other Veterans Administration employees have taken the course, which is still being taught.[70]

No organization in the United States has had a greater influence on plain language than the Document Design Center — through its research, publications, and people.

26. U.S.: Federal-Employee PLAIN Group and the Clinton–Gore Initiatives

Condemnations of U.S.-government writing by federal employees themselves goes back at least to 1966, when John O'Hayre in the Bureau of Land Management wrote a little gem called *Gobbledygook Has Gotta Go*.

Thirty years later, in April 1996, a group of federal employees who were tired of their agencies' bureaucratic writing held the first "Plain English Forum," sponsored by the Office of Management and Budget. The response was overwhelming, and a core group decided to keep meeting. PLAIN stands for Plain Language Action and Information Network.

While PLAIN wasn't the first plain-language initiative in the U.S. federal government, it was the first organized, cross-agency effort — and it caught the eye of the Clinton

---

[70] *See* Susan Kleimann & Melodee Mercer, *Changing a Bureaucracy — One Paragraph at a Time*, 43 Clarity 26 (May 1999) (describing the course).

Administration. In 1997, Vice President Gore asked the group's chair, Annetta Cheek from the Interior Department, to join his National Performance Review and try to spread plain language across the government. In 1998, President Clinton issued his presidential memorandum requiring agencies to use plain language in all new documents.[71] Guidance on how to implement the memo soon followed.[72] Both documents were written mostly by PLAIN.

On June 1, 1998, the same day Clinton issued his memo, Vice President Gore announced his No Gobbledygook Awards program. The awards,[73] which featured before-and-after examples of government writing, received considerable attention from the press and among government employees. Seventeen winners were chosen over the life of the program.

It's remarkable that PLAIN has never received any funding but is still going strong 15 years after it was founded. Its website, www.plainlanguage.gov, is an outstanding resource for plain-language writers from all sectors. PLAIN also conducts short monthly programs and free half-day training sessions — activities that continue to promote the steady growth of interest in plain language by federal agencies.

27. U.S.: Center for Plain Language

In 2003, PLAIN decided that it was time to form a private-sector arm. Mainstays from the group joined with several longtime plain-language practitioners from the private sector,

---

[71] Available at http://www.plainlanguage.gov/whatisPL/govmandates/memo.cfm.

[72] Available at http://www.plainlanguage.gov/howto/guidelines/PresMemoGuidelines.cfm.

[73] *See* http://www.plainlanguage.gov/examples/award_winning/nogobbledygook.cfm.

incorporated in Virginia, and then got federal nonprofit, tax-exempt status as the Center for Plain Language.[74]

The Center's first major activity, in 2005, was to host the fifth conference of the international group PLAIN (see highlight 28). (There are two different PLAINs.) The turnout was huge — 300 people from 16 countries. Since then, the Center has put on at least one event a year, usually a symposium or a workshop.[75] In 2010, the Center began an awards program to present ClearMark awards to outstanding examples of clear communication from government and the private sector, and WonderMark awards to truly bad specimens.[76] Finally, the Center was the driving force behind the momentous Plain Writing Act of 2010 (see highlight 10).

28. Canada: Plain Language Association International

In 1993, responding to a growing interest in plain language by the Canadian government, Cheryl Stephens of Vancouver and Kate Harrison of Winnipeg founded the Plain Language Network. At the time it was Canadian, but now it has grown to become the Plain Language Association InterNational (PLAIN). Before PLAIN came Clarity (see highlight 32). These are the two primary international plain-language organizations — the double engines of activity.

PLAIN's website includes a wealth of resources from around the world.[77] The organization has an active listserv for members.[78] It has held eight conferences and counting, in these cities: Winnipeg (1995), Calgary (1997), Houston (2000), Toronto (2002), Washington, D.C. (2005), Amsterdam (2007),

---

[74] *See* http://centerforplainlanguage.org.

[75] *See* http://centerforplainlanguage.org/topic/events.

[76] *See* http://centerforplainlanguage.org/awards.

[77] *See* http://www.plainlanguagenetwork.org.

[78] http://groups.yahoo.com/group/plainlanguage.

Sydney (2009), and Stockholm (2011). Programs, summaries, and some papers from the conferences are available on PLAIN's website. A fuller assortment of papers from the D.C., Amsterdam, and Sydney conferences appeared in *Clarity* Nos. 55 (May 2006), 59 (May 2008), and 62 (Nov. 2009).[79]

Finally — and notably — PLAIN organized an international working group that has been examining the difficult issues of defining plain language, setting standards, gathering research, certifying practitioners, and strengthening plain-language institutions. The long-awaited working paper was published in *Clarity* No. 64 (Nov. 2010).

29. Canada: Canadian Legal Information Centre and Its Plain Language Centre

In 1973, the Canadian federal government, provincial governments, legal publishers, and professional legal organizations created the Canadian Law Information Council. Its goal was to improve the quality of legal information and the public's access to it. By 1975, CLIC had established the Public Legal Education Committee, a forerunner of many of the public legal-education organizations that now exist in each Canadian province.[80] In 1986, CLIC (under the new name Canadian Legal Information Centre) set up a Plain Language Centre to promote plain English and plain French in legal documents.

CLIC's strength came from being a national nonprofit coalition of lawyers (law societies, bar associations, law faculties), judges, attorneys general, justice ministers, and law publishers. It focused on legal literacy — on making the processes and language of the law clear to the public.

---

[79] Available at http://www.clarity-international.net/pastjournals.html.

[80] For a list, see http://www.cba.org/cba/public/main/info.aspx.

- CLIC commissioned research studies demonstrating that plain language would work in both common law and civil law.[81]
- The Plain Language Centre collected an extensive library of Canadian and international plain-language resources, and shared it across the public and private sectors throughout Canada. For years, people and teams working on plain language were regular borrowers of the library's materials. Upon closing, CLIC deposited its collection partly with the federal government's Human Resources Library and partly with Alberta's Legal Resource Center.
- CLIC invited Robert Eagleson, a plain-language pioneer from Australia, to speak in several major cities in the summer of 1988. Many advocates today credit Dr. Eagleson with sparking their interest.
- The Plain Language Centre developed bilingual training workshops and reworked many legal documents, forms, reports, and audiovisual resources.[82]

In all its activities, CLIC set out to embed plain language in the legal system — as an experiment and a leap of faith. Its funding ceased in 1992, after almost 20 years, but by then CLIC had spread the plain-language message throughout federal and provincial organizations.

---

[81] *See, e.g.*, Nicole Fernbach, *La lisibilité dans la rédaction juridique au Québec* (CLIC 1990) (the first book published about plain French); Gail S. Dykstra, *Plain Language, Legal Documents and Forms* (Canadian Inst. for the Administration of Justice 1987).

[82] *See, e.g.*, Ruth Baldwin, *Clear Writing and Literacy* 32 (rev. 2d ed. 2000) (available at http://library.nald.ca/research/item/5248) (showing a revised residential lease for Toronto's Non-Profit Housing Corporation).

30. Canada: Alberta Law Reform Institute

Since its creation in 1968 as one of Canada's first such institutes, the Alberta Law Reform Institute has prided itself on plain communication. And to encourage plain language in law, the Institute has sponsored several noteworthy projects over the years.

As a demonstration project in the early 1990s, the Institute brought together expert lawyers and plain-language practitioners to create a series of standard documents, including a bank guarantee, will, enduring power of attorney, and parental-consent form.

A decade later, the Institute undertook an exceptional project that lasted seven years — rewriting the 40-year-old rules of civil procedure in Alberta courts. The drafter was David Elliott. The goal: to produce rules that were clear, logically organized, more usable, and more effective. And the Institute delivered.

The new Alberta Rules of Court took effect in November 2010.[83] They largely adopted the Institute's drafting innovations, which included:

- A new (to Alberta) numbering system to support the logical arrangement.
- Succinct descriptive headings for each rule.
- Notes that aid the reader or point to relevant information the reader should be aware of.
- Overview summaries at the beginning of each part giving a high-level description of the part's contents.
- Also at the beginning of each part, a list of terms that have defined meanings in that part.
- Cross-references to a rule that are accompanied by the rule's heading, giving the reader an immediate indication of the nature of the cross-reference — along with a

---

[83] Available at http://www.qp.alberta.ca/1125.cfm.

hypertext link allowing readers to go to the cross-referenced rule if they wish.

Teachers and students, most lawyers and judges, and the general public — along with international observers — have applauded the new rules.

Finally, in 2011 the Institute issued a report on the administration of estates.[84] It, too, was praised for its clarity and for identifying the issues to be resolved. The Institute is committed, as always, to doing everything it can to ensure that the resulting legislation will be equally user-friendly to lawyers and the general public.

31. Canada: Plain Language Service at the Canadian Public Health Association

Since 1997, the Plain Language Service at the Canadian Public Health Association (a voluntary membership organization) has offered plain-language revisions to improve the comprehensibility of health materials for adults with low literacy skills. The work had its origins in the CPHA's groundbreaking national literacy and health program, set up in 1994 to raise awareness about the links between low literacy and adults' access to healthcare services and information. The Plain Language Service became part of that program.

The first manager, Debra Huron, was assigned three goals:

- Revise existing health information or create new plain-language materials for 26 partner organizations in Canada, and for other organizations and government departments.
- Train health professionals to use plain-writing principles.

---

[84] Available at http://www.law.ualberta.ca/alri/docs/rfd022.pdf.

- Create a directory to analyze and showcase examples of plain health information from across North America.[85]

From 1997 to 2000, the Plain Language Service received funding from Canada's National Literacy Secretariat. During that time, the Service revised more than 100 documents, both long and short, and offered plain-language training to its 26 partner organizations as often as requested.

From 2000 to the present, the Service has operated as a self-financing arm within the CPHA. It has worked with dozens of professional groups on their websites and their plain-language projects — for example, revising the certification exam of the Canadian Association of Occupational Therapists to make the process fair for professionals from other countries; and simplifying the training manual for TrainCan Inc.'s food-safety certification program.

The Plain Language Service continues to be a unique venture in the field of health literacy and a model for plain-language work in Canada.

32. UK: Clarity — The International Association Promoting Plain Legal Language

Clarity is the oldest international plain-language organization. It was founded in 1983 by a local-government solicitor, John Walton, who "wonder[ed] if there were other lawyers out there who were equally opposed to archaic, over-complicated legal language."[86] So Walton wrote a letter to the *Law Society Gazette* inviting solicitors and barristers to form a group called Clarity. Twenty-eight founding members accepted, and soon the first newsletter, a four-pager, was printed.

---

[85] Available at http://publications.cpha.ca/products/3-1bk02178.

[86] John Walton, *The Founding of Clarity*, 54 Clarity 4, 5 (Nov. 2005).

Clarity has now grown to about 650 members in 50 countries. It has official representatives in 30 of them, from Lesotho to Hong Kong. Its patrons are Sir Christopher Staughton, retired justice of the British High Court; Michael Kirby, retired justice of the Australian High Court; and Sir Kenneth Keith, a judge on the International Court of Justice. The organization's journal, also called *Clarity*, has grown to a substantial publication of 50–70 pages, appearing twice a year.[87] It's a gold mine of information about plain language around the world — developments in different countries, success stories, practical advice, before-and-after examples, the latest research, strategies for changing ingrained attitudes and carrying out programs, and more. Clarity has held international conferences in Cambridge (2002), Boulogne (2005), Mexico City (2008), and Lisbon (2010). Another is set for Washington, D.C., in 2012. Selected papers from Boulogne were published in *Clarity* Nos. 54 (Nov. 2005) and 55 (May 2006), from the Mexico City conference in No. 61 (May 2009), and from the Lisbon conference in No. 65 (May 2011).

The journal was edited for many years by Mark Adler. He was followed by Phil Knight, Michèle Asprey, and the current editor, Julie Clement. It is the indispensable international journal of plain language.

33. UK: Plain English Campaign and Plain Language Commission

On July 26, 1979, some 12 weeks after Margaret Thatcher became Prime Minister, two northern mavericks with a messianic streak descended on London in a hired transit van full of cardboard boxes trussed up in symbolic red tape. Martin Cutts and Chrissie Maher marched into Parliament

---

[87] Back issues are available at http://www.clarity-international.net/pastjournals.html.

Square, fixed a shredding machine to a collapsible table, and, overlooked by the citadels of state power and bureaucracy, proceeded to destroy a heap of official forms written in gobbledygook. Thus was the Plain English Campaign born in a fanfare of publicity that, long before the dawn of e-mail and the Internet, echoed around the world.

Cutts and Maher gave passersby and journalists a leaflet about their aims: "The Plain English Campaign wants to stop the hardship, confusion and waste caused by complicated forms. All official forms and leaflets should be written in plain, simple English. So should all agreements about money, goods and services that are signed by members of the public." The stunt ended only when a police officer intoned a chunk of verbiage from the Metropolitan Police Act 1839 outlawing demonstrations in the square while Parliament was sitting. Its complexity made the protesters' point perfectly.

At the outset, the cofounders were just about broke and operated from their homes in Salford and Manchester. To make some money, they started running training courses and rewriting documents in plainer English. They also attracted media attention through the annual Plain English Awards (beginning in 1980), which gave prizes for excellent documents and brickbats for bad ones. Government chiefs (including future Prime Minister John Major) turned up to accept trophies from presenters — among them the esteemed judge Lord Denning and the actor Julie Walters. A few brave souls also came to collect their booby prizes, which in one year were bags of the best Lancashire tripe.

Words were never the campaigners' sole focus. At the heart of their call for clarity were good typography and the importance of testing documents on consumers. They sought advice from typographers Ernest Hoch and Mike Frost, as well as practical-minded academics such as Patricia Wright, James Hartley, and Rob Waller.

The Campaign also gained strong support from the National Consumer Council, a government-backed research agency. The Council began to lobby energy and water companies for clearer consumer information and later asked Cutts and Maher to write *Small Print* (1983), a report about obscure consumer contracts, with examples of how to write them better. In 1984, the Council published a draft plain-language law. It became one of the catalysts for the European Community's Unfair Contract Terms Directive of 1993 (see highlight 11).

The Campaign's mix of serious work, publicity, and mockery has influenced many national- and local-government agencies to reform their documents along plain-language principles and commit themselves to using plain language when writing to customers.

More than 30 years later, both cofounders are still active in the plain-language field, although a rift in 1989 led their paths to diverge.

Maher remains the matriarch of Plain English Campaign Limited, which has published (among other books) *Utter Drivel* (1994) and *Language on Trial* (1996). Back issues of its newsletter, *Plain English*, are available on its website.[88] Among other honors, Maher was appointed OBE (Officer of the British Empire) by Queen Elizabeth II.

In 1994, Cutts founded and still heads Plain Language Commission. He has written two well-regarded books: *The Oxford Guide to Plain English* (3d ed. 2009) and *Lucid Law* (2d ed. 2000), which showed how a British act of Parliament could be rewritten and redesigned on plain-language principles. Both books and the company's newsletter, *Pikestaff*, are available on its website.[89]

Several state-funded initiatives on plain language have fallen by the wayside, but Plain English Campaign and Plain Language Commission are still going strong. For both, the main earners have been training courses and paid-for

---

[88] http://plainenglish.co.uk.
[89] http://www.clearest.co.uk.

certification marks that organizations add to documents and websites meeting their criteria — respectively the Crystal Mark (launched in 1990, appearing on 20,000 documents) and the Clear English Standard (launched in 1994, appearing on 16,000 documents). These logos help keep the idea of plain words in the public mind.

34. European Union: Fight the Fog and the Clear Writing Campaign

Fight the Fog was started in 1998 by Emma Wagner and other English translators in the European Commission — the executive body responsible for the day-to-day running of the European Union. The founders feared that the EU was not communicating its message to the public. Their campaign at first concentrated on the use of English in the European Commission and included a booklet tailored to in-house writers — *How to Write Clearly* (1998) — as well as lectures, training sessions, a website, and even a campaign song. It had two main accomplishments:

- The creation of an editing service at the European Commission to improve in-house texts before publication, and a web-editing service specifically for web material on the EU's Europa portal.
- The eventual introduction of citizens' summaries of EU policy documents and legislation (an idea that originally came from Martin Cutts[90]).

The campaign was relaunched in 2010 as the new multilingual Clear Writing Campaign, which targets writing in any language (not just English) and includes a range of in-house

---

[90] *See* Martin Cutts, *Clarifying Eurolaw* 6, 22 (2001) (recommending and illustrating citizens' summaries); Martin Cutts & Emma Wagner, *Clarifying EC Regulations* 5–6, 20 (2002) (doing the same) (both publications available at www.clearest.co.uk).

activities — a survey, conferences, special training courses, and a website with an online tutorial. What's more, there's a new version of *How to Write Clearly*, available for free online in all 23 official languages of the EU — a number that makes it one of a kind.[91] The aim is to reach out to all writers at the Commission.

In November 2010, the Clear Writing team held a conference in Brussels on "Clear Writing Throughout Europe," with speakers from seven EU countries describing their national activities and offering advice to the Commission. The proceedings were published in 2011.[92]

And the campaign song? Yes, the new Clear Writing Campaign has one too, called "Good News — Clarity's a-Coming," available online.[93]

35. Nordic Countries: Language Councils

All the Nordic countries have their own government agencies or state-funded groups devoted to language matters: the Danish Language Council, the Institute for the Languages of Finland, the Árni Magnússon Institute for Icelandic Studies, the Language Council of Norway, and the Language Council of Sweden. Most of these councils were founded in the middle of the twentieth century, and they have been cooperating ever since. They held their first Nordic plain-language conference in 1998.

The councils have published extensively, but only those items with an available English translation are cited in the footnotes. And titles are given in English, with apologies for the monolingualism.

---

[91] http://ec.europa.eu/translation/writing/clear_writing/how_to_write_clearly_en.pdf.

[92] http://bookshop.europa.eu/en/clear-writing-throughout-europe-pbHC3111150/.

[93] http://www.youtube.com/watch?v=sxzU2UH9j_I.

Denmark:

In 1969, the Danish Language Council staff participated in writing the Ministry of Justice's guidelines on the language of laws and regulations. These guidelines were the beginning of plain-language work in Denmark. They were especially influential in identifying textual features that readers find difficult.

Much more recently, the Council played an active role in writing two national reports on the Danish language, *Language at Stake* (2003) and *Language in Time* (2008). Among other things, the reports assessed the clarity of language used by public institutions and private organizations.

In the last few years, the Council has focused on developing plain language as a research field. In 2012–2013, the Council will house a postdoctoral project testing whether traditional plain-language guidelines actually result in better understanding by readers.

Finland:

Public authorities and the Institute for the Languages of Finland have collaborated on plain-language work since the 1970s.[94] The government has established ten positions in the Institute for plain-language experts, who offer consulting and training to private companies and public bodies. The Institute has also published several style guides, it researches plain language, and it devotes part of its website to describing its plain-language activities.[95] The Institute's experts have participated in two important plain-language projects: the

---

[94] For the history of that work, see Aino Piehl, *Finland Makes Its Statutes Intelligible: Good Intentions and Practicalities*, in *Obscurity and Clarity in the Law* 151 (Anne Wagner & Sophie Cacciaguidi-Fahy eds., Ashgate 2008) (available at http://www.kotus.fi/files/2075/Obscurity_and_Clarity_in_the_Law.pdf).

[95] http://www.kotus.fi/index.phtml?l=en&s=4305.

Better Regulation Program,[96] whose goal is to promote better lawmaking and clearer statutes, and Straight to the Point,[97] which aims to make a database of Swedish model texts for local authorities.

In addition, the Institute was actively involved in bringing about two Finnish plain-language statutes, in 1982 and a replacement in 2003. The current statute requires all public authorities to use "appropriate, clear and comprehensible language" in both national languages, Finnish and Swedish.[98]

Iceland:

The Árni Magnússon Institute for Icelandic Studies gives advice on language to individuals and institutions by phone and e-mail.

Iceland does not yet have systematic, organized plain-language work. But there are several initiatives within government offices, Parliament, and a number of public agencies to make texts as clear and comprehensible as possible. One example is a book by the ministries and Parliament called *Handbook on Preparing and Finalizing Draft Legislation* (2007). The new Language Act, passed by Parliament in 2011, states in section 10 that the language used by state and local authorities should be "simple and clear." This new law may well become the basis for organized plain-language work in Iceland.

Norway:

Although the government has undertaken several plain-language initiatives over the years, in 2005 Parliament established a permanent five-member language service

---

[96] *See id.* (containing a summary of the program and a link to a conference presentation).

[97] *See* http://www.localfinland.fi/en/association/research/to-the-point/ Pages/default.aspx (also containing a summary).

[98] Administrative Procedure Act 434/2003, § 9 (available at http://www. finlex.fi/fi/laki/kaannokset/2003/en20030434.pdf).

charged with promoting better and clearer language in government agencies. The service is a part of the Language Council of Norway. Along with other work, the service offers training courses for public-sector employees and evaluates the clarity and correctness of important public documents, such as laws, regulations, and other publications intended for a broad audience.

In 2008, the Ministry of Government Administration, Reform and Church Affairs asked the Agency for Public Management and eGovernment (called Difi) to promote clearer public documents. And Difi has since worked with the Language Council to establish and run the project on plain language in the civil service (see highlight 20).

Sweden:

The Language Council of Sweden has a network of plain-language contacts in about 400 Swedish public agencies and municipalities, all of which are encouraged to initiate plain-language work. The Council offers seminars on how to start and maintain projects; gives lectures at public agencies; publishes handbooks, style guides, and a plain-language bulletin; provides a plain-language test online; and awards a yearly prize, the Plain Language Crystal.[99] Some of this work was previously done by the Plain Swedish Group (see highlight 36) before the government assigned it to the Council.

In 2005, Parliament decided on a "Best Language" policy for Sweden. Its goals included making public-sector language "cultivated, simple and comprehensible."[100] That goal — "clear and comprehensible official texts" — was said to be a "precondition for a living democracy."[101]

---

[99] *See* http://www.sprakradet.se/plain_language.

[100] *See* http://www.regeringen.se/content/1/c6/13/16/05/5cbb31a6.pdf.

[101] *Id.*

Then in 2009, Parliament passed a Language Act based on this policy.[102] And the Language Council is charged with carrying out the policy and monitoring progress. As a first step, the Council has published guidelines, *The Language Act in Practice — Guidelines on the Interpretation of the Law*, and distributed them to all public agencies and organizations.

36. Sweden: Division for Legal and Linguistic Draft Revision, and the Plain Swedish Group

Imagine a country in which every statute has to pass through a government division that revises for plain language — and without whose approval the law cannot be sent to the printer. That country is Sweden, and the division is the Division for Legal and Linguistic Draft Revision.

The story of plain language in the Swedish government is well told in two articles in the journal *Clarity*.[103] The history goes back at least as far as 1967, when a government booklet called *Language in Acts and Other Legislation* set out remarkably progressive (for governments, at least) guidelines for writing clear and simple statutes. In 1976, the government hired its first language expert. And the Linguistic Division was formed in the early 1980s. It now consists of five linguists and five legal advisers devoted to ensuring that laws "are as easy as possible to read and understand."[104] Besides revising draft laws, the linguistic team tries to influence how legislation is developed by holding training sessions for legislative drafters, writing handbooks and guidelines,[105] and giving

---

[102] Available at http://regeringen.se/content/1/c6/13/81/33/c424146c.pdf.

[103] Barbro Ehrenberg-Sundin, *Plain Language in Sweden*, 33 Clarity 16 (July 1995); Barbro Ehrenberg-Sundin, *The Swedish Government Promotes Clear Drafting*, 47 Clarity 3 (May 2002).

[104] Ehrenberg-Sundin, *Plain Language in Sweden, supra* n. 103, at 17.

[105] *E.g.*, *The Black List*, SB PM 2011:1 (4th ed.); *How to Draft Regulations*, Ds 1998:43 (2d ed.) (neither available in English).

advice by telephone or e-mail to legal drafters in all the government ministries.

In 1993, the Swedish government appointed a committee, the Plain Swedish Group (Klarspråksgruppen), to draw on the work and experience of the Linguistic Division and encourage government authorities throughout Sweden to embrace plain language. The Group's activities have included the following:

- Arranging more than 40 plain-language conferences.
- Editing a plain-language bulletin.
- Providing useful information at the government's plain-language website.[106]
- Awarding the yearly Plain Swedish Crystal to deserving government projects.

All these activities are now being carried out at the Swedish Language Council (see highlight 35).

Finally, Sweden was probably the first country to create a university-level degree in plain language. In 1978, Stockholm University set up a program in Swedish Language Consultancy. Graduates from that program are in demand in both the public and private sectors.

In so many ways, Sweden provides a model for the rest of the world.

37. Australia: Law Reform Commission of Victoria

The debate over plain legal language in Australia began on May 7, 1985, when Attorney General Jim Kennan made a Ministerial Statement called *Plain English Legislation* in Victoria's Parliament.[107] In his statement, Kennan announced

---

[106] http://www.sprakradet.se/klarspråk (as now maintained by the Swedish Language Council).

[107] Hansard, Legislative Council 432 (1985).

various changes, including (1) a requirement that each legislative bill include a statement of its "purpose/objectives," and (2) a directive that *must* replace *shall* when "used to impose an obligation."

A few months later, Kennan referred the topic of plain language in legislation and government communications to the Law Reform Commission of Victoria (later abolished and replaced by the Victorian Law Reform Commission). David St L Kelly, the chair of the Commission, drove its plain-language work.

The Commission produced two now-legendary reports: *Plain English and the Law* (1987; repr. 1990) and *Access to Law: The Structure and Format of Legislation* (1990). These reports made a powerful case for plain legal language and have been widely cited. As appendixes to the first report, the Commission prepared demonstration rewrites of existing documents:

- The Takeovers Code (the law governing one company's takeover of another).
- A standard mortgage produced by the Law Institute of Victoria (equivalent to a U.S. state bar association).
- Various government letters and notices.

The Commission also pushed for plain language in its work on other topics. For example, in its report on equal-opportunity law, it produced a plain-language rewrite of Victoria's Equal Opportunity Act (1984). The key to the Commission's winning the debate was that it arranged for its rewrites to be approved by lawyers who were experts in the relevant fields.

Gradually, the quality of the Commission's arguments, together with the practical and contemporary nature of its demonstration rewrites, caused most of the legal profession to fall silent in its opposition to plain language.

38. Australia: Centre for Plain Legal Language

The Law Foundation Centre for Plain Legal Language was established at Sydney University's Faculty of Law in 1990. Its founding directors were two academics from the University: Dr. Robert Eagleson, a linguist, and Peter Butt, a lawyer. The Centre was funded by a substantial grant that Dr. Eagleson obtained from the Law Foundation of New South Wales.

The Centre undertook research into the use of plain English in law, in Australia and elsewhere. It also produced several substantial legal documents and conducted training programs in plain legal language for judges, practicing lawyers, and law students. Three of its activities merit special mention:

- A monthly "Words and Phrases" column in the New South Wales *Law Society Journal*. Each month, the Centre chose a traditional legal word or phrase (such as *joint and several* and *right, title, and interest*), researched the interpretation that the term had received in the courts, and then suggested a plain-English equivalent that would capture the legal nuances of the original.[108]

- Work on the design of legislation, a joint project with the New South Wales Parliamentary Counsel's Office (see highlight 23).

- Research on the economic benefits of plain-English documents — the subject of much anecdotal but (at that time) limited evidence. The resulting publication demonstrated their greater efficiency for all concerned.[109]

---

[108] The columns were collected and published as *Law Words* (Ctr. for Plain Legal Language 1995) (available at http://www.clarity-international.net/downloads/Law%20Words.pdf).

[109] *See* Gordon Mills & Mark Duckworth, *The Gains from Clarity* (1996) (cited in part 5 of this book, summary 14).

The Centre closed in 1996 — after six very productive years.

39. New Zealand: Law Commission and the Parliamentary Counsel Office

For decades, New Zealand has been committed to plain language in legislative drafting, and the two main forces have been the Law Commission and the Parliamentary Counsel Office.

The Law Commission was established in 1985 to (among other things) "propose ways of making legislation as understandable and accessible as practicable."[110] To that end, the Commission produced three influential reports (the second and third are available for purchase online[111]):

- Report No. 17, *A New Interpretation Act to Avoid "Prolixity and Tautology"* (1990).
- Report No. 27, *The Format of Legislation* (1993).
- Report No. 35, *Legislation Manual: Structure and Style* (1996).

These reports were full of advice and examples on all aspects of plain language. One piece of guidance: "Use *must* in preference to *shall*: it is clear and definite, and commonly understood."[112]

These three reports helped set the stage for the ten-year project to rewrite New Zealand's entire tax act. The project

---

[110] Law Comm'n, Report No. 17, *A New Interpretation Act to Avoid "Prolixity and Tautology"* ix (1990).

[111] http://www.lawcom.govt.nz/publications.

[112] *Legislation Manual: Structure and Style* 43.

was carried out jointly by the Parliamentary Counsel Office and a drafting unit within the Inland Revenue Department.[113]

Over the years, the Law Commission has found an ally in the Parliamentary Counsel Office.[114] The Office's drafting manual adopts many recommendations contained in the Law Commission's third report above. And since January 1, 2000, all New Zealand statutes and regulations have been printed in a new format that reflects many recommendations in the Commission's second report. That report, along with two Australian reports produced in the 1990s (see highlight 23), changed the look of legislation in these two countries.

40. Commonwealth Countries: Commonwealth Association of Legislative Counsel

The Commonwealth Association of Legislative Counsel was established at a meeting of law drafters held in September 1983. It seeks "to promote cooperation . . . among Commonwealth persons and others who are or have been engaged in legislative drafting . . . and to promote the use of effective legislative drafting practices and techniques."[115]

Since its founding, CALC has held ten conferences in conjunction with Commonwealth Law Conferences. Over the last 15 years or so, papers touching on plain language and highlighting other advances in drafting techniques have been

---

[113] For a description of the process and some of the drafting improvements, see Margaret Nixon, *Rewriting the Income Tax Act*, 52 Clarity 22 (Nov. 2004).

[114] *See* http://www.pco.parliament.govt.nz/clear-drafting (setting out "principles of clear drafting"); *see also* George Tanner, *Imperatives in Drafting Legislation: A Brief New Zealand Perspective*, 52 Clarity 7 (Nov. 2004) (describing the Office's approach to legislation and its accomplishments).

[115] CALC Constitution 4(1)(a), (c) (as consolidated on April 10, 2009) (available at http://www.opc.gov.au/calc/docs/CALCConstitution.pdf).

a central part of CALC's conferences. And CALC's flagship publication, *The Loophole*, has published many articles and papers on issues related to plain language.[116]

CALC now has over 1,000 members spread across the Commonwealth and beyond. While its founding was not driven by plain-language considerations, it has helped promote plainer drafting across the world and share knowledge on how to go about it.

---

[116] *See* http://www.opc.gov.au/calc/index.htm; for a separate report on the state of plain-language drafting internationally, see Office of Scottish Parliamentary Counsel, *Plain Language and Legislation* (2006) (available at http://scotland.gov.uk/Resource/Doc/93488/0022476.pdf).

PART FIVE

The Extraordinary Benefits

To most people, the benefits of plain language are intuitive. If readers understand plain language better, then no doubt they'll like it better than the dense, impersonal prose of most public and legal documents. And because they understand it better, they'll make fewer mistakes in dealing with it, have fewer questions, and ultimately save time and money — for themselves and for the writer's company or agency.

There is, in fact, much informal evidence to this effect. Take, for example, four older publications called *The Productivity of Plain English*,[1] *How Plain English Works for Business: Twelve Case Studies*,[2] *Plain English for Better Business*,[3] and *Plain English at Work*.[4] They are full of testimonials from officials at trade associations (American Council of Life Insurance, American Gas Association) and at businesses (Shell Oil, Target Stores, Pfizer, Sentry Insurance, Bank of America, General Motors, Royal Sun Alliance in Australia). These officials offer the evidence of their senses. They can see and feel the change that plain language makes:

---

[1] Office of Consumer Affairs, U.S. Dep't of Commerce (1983).
[2] Office of Consumer Affairs, U.S. Dep't of Commerce (1984).
[3] Council of Better Business Bureaus, Tenth Annual Washington Forum: A Summary of Proceedings (1986).
[4] Commonwealth of Australia (1996).

- It streamlines procedures and paperwork, makes it easier to train staff, and increases staff productivity and morale.
- It reduces confusion, complaints, and claims, and it improves customer satisfaction.
- It increases sales and raises the company's standing in the marketplace.

But — and here is the irony — for the very reason that these benefits are so apparent, companies and agencies are not inclined to try to measure them. Why spend more money to study how much money the company was losing and is now saving? Rather, the company knows from experience that a document is causing trouble; somebody revises the document; and if the trouble seems to go away, the company calls it good.

To do otherwise would require a cost-benefit study, which is inherently difficult. You have to collect before-and-after data about the document. How many errors was the staff having to correct, or how many phone calls was it getting? How long did it take, on average, to fix the error or answer the call or process the document? (Sometimes you have to make a conservative estimate.) Then you have to figure out how much the staff's time was worth. Then you have to calculate how much it cost to develop the new document. Finally, you have to get parallel data for the new document. And after all that, you still can't be sure that you'll realize similar savings by converting a different document into plain language. There are too many kinds of documents and too many variables.

Despite these difficulties and limitations, though, studies have been done. Most of them have been done not by accountants, not by managers, but by persons with a concern for writing — consultants, technical writers, and proponents of plain language. If numbers are needed to make the case for clear writing, then we've got numbers.

I've divided the studies, somewhat artificially, into two main categories. The first one reflects the tangible cost benefits of plain language for the writer's company or agency. The second one confirms the many benefits of plain language for the reader. Of course, the benefits for the reader usually produce the benefits for the writer's organization.

For most of the studies, especially the more recent ones, the authors have been kind enough to review my summary. The savings calculations in the first group were accurate at the time of the study. To the extent that projects were involved, most have now ended, and it's hard to know whether the revised letter or form or manual is still in use, or even whether some of the organizations are still around. Nor is that worth checking into. The time of the studies doesn't matter. The point is to demonstrate the extraordinary range and size of potential benefits.

Behold, then, the 50 studies and reports that follow. Just browse through them, and know they're on hand as needed to make the case. Again, those in the first category show that plain language — in its full scope — can save organizations a ton of money. Those in the second category cement what we probably knew all along: readers strongly prefer plain language in public and legal documents, they understand it better than bureaucratic and legalistic style, they find it faster and easier to use, they are more likely to comply with it, and they are much more likely to read it in the first place.

SAVING TIME AND MONEY

There is an order to the summaries in this first category: 1–14 demonstrate savings to government; 15–21, savings to business; and 22–23, savings to consumers. As you would expect, these savings take many forms: fewer phone calls to the organization, less time needed by consumers and staff to deal with an item, fewer errors all around, a better response rate to letters and inquiries, an increased rate of timely payments, less need for follow-up, decreased printing and mailing costs, and more informed decisions of all kinds by consumers.

In all this variety, though, two themes stand out. First, a small saving on a single act produces huge numbers when that same act is performed repeatedly on a high-volume document. Second, an investment in plain language will repay itself many times over.

Another point about this first category: the studies don't directly measure readers' comprehension, as many of those in the second category do. But they certainly measure it indirectly. That is, the various kinds of savings — fewer calls, fewer errors, and the like — surely flow from better understanding of the documents. What else could it be? So these studies form an additional body of evidence based on testing the actual users of real-world documents.

1. U.S.: Federal Communications Commission — Regulations[5]

When the FCC's regulations for citizens-band radios (remember those?) were written in legalese, the agency needed five full-time staff members to answer questions from the public. In 1977 or 1978, the FCC rewrote the regulations in plain language and was able to reassign the five staff members.

Incidentally, in the years that followed, there was not a single reported case implicating the plain language in those regulations. So much for the fear that plain language will create litigation. If anything, it probably decreases litigation.

Below is a before-and-after example that shows the difference just in headings, which are vitally important to readers who come to documents wanting to find answers to their questions. (The examples are from Title 47 of the *Code of Federal Regulations*.)

Before:

§ 95.455   Authorized frequencies.

§ 95.457   Policy governing the availability of frequencies.

§ 95.437   Limitations on antenna structures.

§ 95.511   Transmitter service and maintenance.

§ 95.613   Transmitter power.

§ 95.509   External radio frequency power amplifiers prohibited.

After:

§ 95.407   On what channels may I operate?

§ 95.408   How high may I put my antenna?

§ 95.409   What equipment may I use at my CB station?

---

[5] *Plain Language Pays*, 63 Simply Stated (newsletter of American Institutes for Research) 1, 4 (Feb. 1986).

§ 95.410   How much power may I use?

§ 95.411   May I use power amplifiers?

2. U.S.: Veterans Benefits Administration — Form Letters[6]

The Veterans Benefits Administration, a part of the Department of Veterans Affairs, has for more than 15 years dedicated itself to a program called "Reader-Focused Writing." Staff writers have been trained in plain language, and countless letters have been revised.

One early project was conducted at the agency's regional offices in Jackson, Mississippi, and Little Rock, Arkansas. In February 1991, a consultant began training the VBA's letter-writers. As part of the training, the writers revised some of the VBA's form letters. To make sure that the new form letters worked, project leaders tested them in two ways: through cued-response protocol tests, in which veterans read the letters aloud and tried to paraphrase them at certain spots; and through focus groups. The new letters were then further revised.

This project bears witness to the fundamental truth that good writing will improve the content: "In revising these letters, the writers do much more than merely simplify sentences and shorten words. They rethink the entire letter. Often their revisions result in radically changed content to better meet the readers' needs."[7]

The agency then tried to measure the results. In Jackson, five benefits counselors were asked how many phone calls

---

6   Reva Daniel & William Schuetz, VA's "Writing for Real People" Pays Off (unpublished report, May 1994); see also Reva Daniel, Revising Letters to Veterans, 42 Technical Communication 69 (1995) (containing most of the same information, but not the estimated dollar savings and the sample letters cited in the report).

7   Daniel & Schuetz, supra n. 6, at 6-4; Daniel, supra n. 6, at 70.

they received about a selected old letter in one year and about the new letter in the next year. The counselors hadn't kept a log, but their individual estimates were quite consistent. (They figured calls per month, which were then multiplied by 12.) Results for the old letter: 750 sent out and 1,128 calls received. For the new letter: 710 sent out and 192 calls received. The project coordinator estimated that the savings on this *one letter alone*, if adopted at offices nationwide, would be more than $40,000 a year. And remember that the agency sends out thousands of different letters.

Below are the old and new letters. Notice just some of the improvements in the new one: it provides a context; it divides up the information and uses headings; it uses more white space; it's simple and direct ("Send us . . . ."); it cuts out unnecessary detail, like the comment about not having to get a new examination and the citation to the *United States Code*; and it uses contractions.

Before:

Dear ———————:

Please furnish medical evidence in support of your pension claim. The best evidence to submit would be a report of a recent examination by your personal physician, or a report from a hospital or clinic that has treated you recently. The report should include complete findings and diagnoses of the condition which renders you permanently and totally disabled. It is not necessary for you to receive an examination at this time. We only need a report from a doctor, hospital, or clinic that has treated you recently.

This evidence should be submitted as soon as possible, preferably within 60 days. If we do not receive this information within 60 days from the date of this letter, your claim will be denied. Evidence must be received in the Department of Veterans Affairs within one year from the date of this letter; otherwise, benefits, if entitlement is established, may not be paid prior to the date of its receipt. SHOW VETERAN'S FULL NAME AND VA FILE NUMBER ON ALL EVIDENCE SUBMITTED.

Privacy Act Information: The information requested by this letter is authorized by existing law (38 U.S.C. 210 (c)(1)) and is considered necessary and relevant to determine entitlement to maximum benefits applied for under the law. The information submitted may be disclosed outside the Department of Veterans Affairs only as permitted by law.

_____

Adjudication Officer

After:

Dear _____:

We have your claim for a pension. Our laws require us to ask you for more information. The information you give us will help us decide whether we can pay you a pension.

What We Need

Send us a medical report from a doctor or clinic that you visited in the past six months. The report should show why you can't work.

Please take this letter and the enclosed Guide to your doctor.

When We Need It

We need the doctor's report by <u>January 28, 1992</u>. We'll have to turn down your claim if we don't get the report by that date.

Your Right to Privacy

> The information you give us is private. We might have to give out this information in a few special cases. But we will not give it out to the *general public* without your permission. We've attached a form which explains your privacy rights.
>
> If you have any questions about this letter, you may call us at 1-800-827-1000. The call is free.
>
> Sincerely,

> _____

> Enclosures: Doctor's Guide, Your Privacy Rights

3. U.S.: Veterans Benefits Administration — Form Letters[8]

In 1998, VBA tested the results of another new letter — a letter to 320,000 veterans who had not updated the named beneficiary on their government life insurance for at least 40 years. The letter asked veterans to complete a new form that could be scanned into a database. In previous mailings of an old letter, the response rate had never been better than 43%. The response to the revised letter was 66%.

In 1999, VBA sent essentially the same revised letter to about 2 million veterans whose beneficiary forms were less than 40 years old. The response rate again improved to around 65%.

So what were the benefits? In 1999, VBA calculated that because of the extra time (at least 20 minutes) it took to

8 E-mails from Melodee Mercer, VBA Insurance Specialist & Writing Instructor, to the author (Dec. 14 & 15, 1999; Feb. 16, 2000) (including undated Beneficiary Solicitation Letter summary).

identify and locate beneficiaries if the old form had not been updated, it would save $8.68 using an updated form. The improved response rate — from 43% to 65% — among 2,320,000 veterans (320,000 + 2,000,000) produced an additional 510,400 updated forms (22% × 2,320,000). At $8.68 per updated form, VBA's revised letter saved an estimated $4,430,000.

For letters that go out by the thousands and hundreds of thousands and millions, the total cost savings from small individual gains can be staggering.

4. U.S.: Naval Officers — Business Memos[9]

In the next section, summary 41 concerns a 1989 study of naval officers who read a business memo that was written either in a plain style or in a bureaucratic style. Officers who read the plain memo, besides having significantly higher comprehension, took 17% to 23% less time to read it and felt less need to reread it.

In another study two years later, the authors put dollar figures on their results. They determined the average hourly pay for a naval officer. They then constructed two scenarios: one used a very low estimate of how many pages of reports and memos an officer reads in a year; the other used a more likely estimate. In each case, the authors applied the reading-time differences, in seconds per page, from their original study.

Under the first scenario, the Navy would save from $27 to $37 million worth of time each year if its officers routinely read plain writing. Under the second scenario, the savings would total $53 to $73 million. Even more remarkable are the savings if all naval personnel (not just officers) read plain documents: $250 to $350 million a year.

---

[9] James Suchan & Robert Colucci, *The High Cost of Bureaucratic Written Communications*, 34 Business Horizons 68 (Mar.–Apr. 1991).

That is just one kind of cost benefit measured across just one government agency.

5. U.S.: State of Washington — Consumer Documents[10]

In 2001, the Washington Department of Labor and Industries began a "Plain Talk" project to rewrite 100 of its form letters into plain language. Some other agencies followed suit, and in 2003 the Department of Revenue rewrote a letter that tripled the number of businesses paying a commonly ignored use tax. In just one year, the letter produced $800,000 more in revenue than the department had projected.

Results like this led the governor to sign a "Plain Talk" Executive Order in 2005. In the years that followed, 35 cabinet agencies adopted Plain Talk programs, at least 7,500 employees were trained in plain language, more than 2,000 letters and forms were rewritten, and six major websites were overhauled. Each agency had an assigned Plain Talk leader; the leaders formed committees to develop guidelines, measurements, and awards; and each agency submitted a yearly progress report to the governor. Unfortunately, the Plain Talk program began losing momentum in 2009 because of budget troubles. Never mind that the seminal use-tax letter cost 1 cent for every dollar collected.

Here are more success stories from that program's brief run:

---

[10] Dana Howard Botka, Workshop Slides, *Washington State: Where We "Plain Talk,"* http://www.plainlanguage.gov/news/PLAINPresentation4-1-08.ppt (Apr. 1, 2008); Dana Howard Botka, Workshop Slides, *In a "Self-Serve" Economy: Using Plain Talk to Improve Processes — and Save Money* (Aug. 6, 2009); E-mails from Dana Howard Botka, Manager of Customer Communications, Wash. Dep't of Labor & Industries, to the author (Mar. 16 & July 7, 2010, Mar. 16, 2012).

- The Department of Social and Health Services rewrote letters sent to citizens about their benefits. Before, the agency would send separate letters for each benefit (food stamps, medical, cash assistance), totaling 1.5 million pages per month. The new letter consolidated 12 letters into 1, thus reducing postage by $25,000 annually and probably reducing confusion as well.

- The Department of Labor and Industries developed clearer instructions and explanations for citizens requesting public records. About 10% of people were calling with routine process questions, slowing staff response times. In one year, phone calls dropped by 95%, allowing the staff to reduce its response time from 12 to 8 days. Also, the department was able to withdraw an earlier budget request for two additional employees at $110,000 a year. And the following year, when requests for public records suddenly tripled, the department managed with the same number of staff positions.

- The Department of Revenue wrote clearer instructions to businesses for returning unclaimed property (usually funds) because many were ignoring the old, unclear notice. The new notice increased the response rate from 41% to 76% in one year.

- The Health Care Authority, which administers benefits to state employees, needed to cut costs and call-center wait times by getting more members online. The department wrote clearer instructions for how to start an online account, and those accounts jumped by 8,500, or 30%, in seven months. Even though more people, in general, are going online every day, the increase still exceeded expectations. For each phone inquiry avoided, the department saves $3.50 — or an extra $30,000 annually if each new account goes online just once instead of phoning.

One last example. The Department of Licensing changed a letter about failing to respond to a citation.

Before:

> ON 2-14-03 AT 12:01 AM YOUR DRIVING PRIVILEGE WILL BE SUSPENDED FOR FAILURE TO APPEAR/PAY/COMPLY ON CITATION #409584 RCW 46.20.289. THE SUSPENSION WILL REMAIN IN EFFECT UNTIL NOTIFIED OF REINSTATEMENT BY THIS DEPARTMENT.
>
> TO AVOID SUSPENSION, YOU MUST RE-SOLVE ALL CHARGES ON THIS CITATION WITH THE COURT INDICATED BELOW AND THE DEPARTMENT MUST RECEIVE PROOF FROM THE COURT BEFORE 02-14-03 THAT THE CHARGE(S) HAVE BEEN RESOLVED. QUESTIONS REGARDING THE CITATION AND/OR FINE SHOULD BE DIRECTED TO THE COURT LISTED BELOW.

After:

> **On 2-14-2003 at 12:01 a.m. your driving privilege will be suspended.**
>
> The Court has notified us that you failed to respond, pay, appear, or comply with the terms of the citation listed below.
>
> | Citation # | Violation Date | Reason for Citation |
> |---|---|---|
> | 000000 | 10-6-2002 | No valid license |
>
> **What do I have to do to avoid suspension of my driving privileges?**
>
> 1. Contact the court below to find out what you must do to take care of this citation. . . .

After the change, the department's hotline busy signals dropped by 95%, allowing 850 more people to reach the hotline each day and freeing up three employees to help customers in other ways.

6. U.S.: Arizona Department of Revenue — Form Letters[11]

In 2006, the Arizona Department of Revenue began a Plain Talk program inspired by the Washington state program (summary 5). The department put together a team of employees from different divisions, began training writers, and began rewriting form letters. By the time the program ended in late 2008, the department had rewritten 101 letters, whose readability scores improved (dropped) about one and a half grade levels on average. As in Washington, the program died because so many department employees were laid off during budget cuts.

Urgent message to cutters: plain language saves money in the long run.

To take an example, one division rewrote three related letters to someone who was trying to assert ownership of unclaimed property (stocks, bank accounts, etc.). In 2005 and 2006, the division had received almost 46,000 calls in response to the letters — or 23,000 a year. In 2007, the number dropped to about 5,000 — or 18,000 fewer. What's more, the division was able to process about 30,000 more claims, and the processing time improved from an average of 49 days to 21 days.

---

[11] Amanda J. Crawford, *State Targets Bureaucratese*, Ariz. Republic B-1, B-4 (Jan. 6, 2008) (available at http://www.azcentral.com/news/articles/ 0106plaintalk0106cappage.html); Interview with Nick Buta, Ariz. Dep't of Revenue, Dep't Quality Executive (Nov. 10, 2009) (providing untitled documents containing data about the letters discussed in the text); E-mail from Nick Buta to the author (Aug. 23, 2010).

To take another example, letters to business taxpayers requesting certain action or information were producing responses at a 15% rate. After they were rewritten, the response rate improved to 85%.

7. U.S.: Los Angeles County — Consumer Documents and Phone Messages[12]

The Los Angeles County Department of Consumer Affairs publishes educational materials for consumers — brochures, recorded phone messages, webpages, and form letters. In 2002, the department began looking at how plain language could make these documents more effective. The department hired a professional writer who conducted writing workshops, edited consumer materials, and coached managers in the techniques of plain language.

Here's an example of how their documents changed:

Before:

> In a high-cost loan, a homeowner borrowing $100,000 would be charged upfront fees totaling $10,000 and be subject to an interest rate of 12 percent or higher. There would be a penalty for paying the loan off early. With a good loan, a homeowner with good credit borrowing $100,000 would be charged upfront fees totaling $1,000 and have an interest rate of around 6 percent. There would be no penalty for early payoff.

---

[12] Tim Bissell, *The Plain Language Project at the Department of Consumer Affairs*, Quality Matters (newsletter of Quality & Productivity Comm'n) (Summer 2006).

After:

> A high-cost loan might charge $10,000 for a loan
> of $100,000. It has an interest rate of 12 percent or
> higher. It also charges a fine if you pay the loan off
> early. A good loan might charge $1,000 for a loan of
> $100,000 — if you have good credit. It has an interest
> rate of around 6 percent. There is no fine if you pay
> the loan off early.

Revisions like this one improved readability on the
department's materials by an average of four grade levels —
from 11th to 7th grade. And the recorded phone messages
used in the Small Claims Advisor Program went from grade
level 9.5 to 6.7. Before installing the plain-language messages,
an average of 5,000 callers a month asked to speak with
someone; afterward, that number dropped to 3,500 — a 30%
reduction. This produces an annual savings of more than
$50,000.

8. Canada: Alberta Agriculture, Food, and Rural Development — Forms[13]

A writing consultant, Susan Barylo, began working with
Alberta Agriculture in 1993 to revise its forms. She didn't
just start rewriting; instead, she had a process for gathering
information from a form's "sponsor" within the organization, from every staff member who touched it, including
those who produced and printed it, and from the readers
who filled it in. She asked the sponsor to figure out things
like the form's return rate and error rate and the staff time to
fix errors. And before the final printing, she tested it on at
least seven typical users.

---

[13] Christine Mowat, *Alberta Agriculture Saves Money with Plain
Language*, 38 Clarity 6 (Jan. 1997); Susan Barylo, Handouts for "Plain
Language in Progress 97" Conference (Sept. 25, 1997).

Over three years, Barylo revised 92 of the 700 or so forms in the department's inventory. More than a million copies of those 92 forms are used each year. Her evidence showed that the department is saving at least ten minutes on each new form it receives — which she said is a conservative estimate. Total savings each year for the 92 forms: about Can$3.5 million.

Here's a glimpse at the kinds of savings:

- On a form to request free trees, the error rate fell from 40% to 20%. For each incorrect form, the staff had to call the applicant and clarify the order. The new form saved about 18 days' worth of staff time.

- On a form to apply for an agricultural-society operating grant, the processing time was reduced from 20 minutes to 3 minutes, again saving about 18 days a year.

- On a registration certificate for livestock, less than 40% of the producers updated it as required; now 95% of them update it without any prompting by the staff.

9. UK: British Government — Forms[14]

In 1982, the British government issued a White Paper, *Administrative Forms in Government*, requiring that all departments undertake a continuous and thorough program to eliminate forms whenever possible and to simplify the rest. What followed was probably the most extensive work on forms that any government has ever carried out. In each of the next three years, 1983 through 1985, the Cabinet Office prepared for the Prime Minister a lengthy, detailed report describing the activities of every government department. Those reports are filled with references to forms eliminated,

---

[14] Cabinet Office, Management & Personnel Office, *Review of Administrative Forms: Third Progress Report to the Prime Minister* (1985) (none of these reports had page numbers).

forms revised, money saved, awards won, training accomplished, special units created, tens of thousands of booklets (like *The Word Is . . . Plain English* and *Good Forms Guide*) distributed, and work done by the Plain English Campaign. The items below are mostly from the 1985 report:

- By 1985, the government had scrapped 15,700 types of forms, improved another 21,300, and reviewed another 46,900.

- By 1985, the estimated cost savings to the departments totaled about £9 million.

- The cost of producing the new forms was less than half the money they saved. And most of the production costs were presumably one-time costs, while the forms would continue to save money each year.

- Example: a legalistic "Notice Claiming the Right to Buy," from the Department of Environment. The old form had an error rate of about 60% in one London test borough; the new form reduced the error rate to below 5%.

- Another example: a form called "Duty Free Allowances," from the Department of Customs and Excise. On this form, used for missing or delayed baggage, the error rate was reduced from 55% to 3%. The new form cost £2,500 and saves £33,000 a year in staff time — not to mention 7,500 hours for passengers.

- One more example: a form called "Civilian Travel Claim Form," from the Ministry of Defence. Over 750,000 are filled out each year. The new form cut the error rate by half, the time to complete it by 10%, and the processing time by 15%. It cost £12,000 and saves £400,000 a year in staff time.

- In an independent study for the Department of Health and Social Security, Coopers & Lybrand concluded that the annual cost to the agency of errors on its forms was "of the order of £675 million," that the costs to employers and members of the public were "of similar magnitude," and that the total costs from one common form alone were £3.5 million.[15]

10. UK: Royal Mail — Form[16]

Siegel+Gale, a pioneering American company whose motto declares that "Simple is Smart," has worked with hundreds of clients over the last 40 years to simplify their procedures and documents.

Before Siegel+Gale clarified a redirection-of-mail form for the Royal Mail (the British postal service), there was an 87% error rate when customers filled it out. Royal Mail was spending over £10,000 a week to deal with complaints and to reprocess the incorrect forms. The new form reduced the error rate dramatically, so that Royal Mail saved £500,000 in just the next nine months.

11. Sweden: Agency for Higher Education Services — Online Forms and E-Mail[17]

This agency processes online applications for Sweden's colleges and universities. It is now handling about 800,000 a year.

---

[15] Coopers & Lybrand Associates, Dep't of Health & Social Security, *Forms Effectiveness Study* 1, 30 (July 1984).

[16] Siegel+Gale, *Proposal for [X] Rental Car Company* 25 (Apr. 16, 1997) (internal document summarizing several of the firm's projects, including the Royal Mail project).

[17] Janice Redish & Susan Kleimann, *Plain Language in Government* ___, in *Usability in Government Systems* (Elizabeth Buie & Dianne Murray eds., Morgan Kaufmann) (forthcoming 2012); E-mails from Karin Hansson, Writing Specialist at the Agency for Higher Education Services, to the author (Jan. 31 & Feb. 1, 2012).

In 2009, the agency formed a team to revise 200 pieces of online content and various standard e-mails sent during the application process. Each team member spent about two hours a week on the project. The team first reviewed the entire application process and what readers need to know. In revising, they added headings, moved the most important information to the beginning, added information on how to ask questions and what to do if something is wrong, omitted unnecessary information, and put instructions in numbered lists.

An example of online content (translated from Swedish):

Before:

> If you already have a user account with your Swedish civic registration number, do not create a new account. Please contact University Studies in Sweden [link] if you need assistance. You will be able to submit an application, follow your application, change your address and reply to the notification of selection results here at studera.nu. However, you cannot access your qualifications. This requires that you create an account with a Swedish civic registration number.
>
> If you have non-disclosable personal details [link] you must apply by mail directly to VHS, PO Box 24070, 104 50 Stockholm, and write "non-disclosable personal details" on the application form. If you apply via the internet, all the information in your application will be available to the public.

After:

> **Do you have personal details you do not want to disclose?**
> To avoid making the personal details in your application available to everyone, you must apply by submitting an application form directly to VHS, PO Box 24070, 104 50 Stockholm. Write "non-disclosable

personal details" on the application form. Read more about <u>non-disclosable personal details</u> [link].

Already have an account with a Swedish civic registration number?
Then you must use it and not create a new account.

Any questions?
Use the <u>contact form</u> [link] to ask a question to University Studies in Sweden.

The team estimated that the revisions reduced the cost of operating the call center by over 20% in 2010. The agency had budgeted almost 8 million kronor based on the expected number of calls and e-mails to the private company it contracts with. But it paid 6.3 million kronor. The only explanation for the reduced calls and e-mails was the improved documents.

12. New Zealand: Ministry of Internal Affairs — Form[18]

The Ministry enlisted the help of Siegel+Gale's New Zealand affiliate to redesign the application for New Zealand citizenship. The old application consisted of 14 badly typed and poorly photocopied forms. The design team chunked the information into manageable units, reorganized them in a logical sequence, eliminated unnecessary detail, translated into plain English, and presented the material in an attractive, functional design. The team's practice was to always "take into account the needs of the end user" — not only the customer but also the staff that handles the forms.[19]

---

[18] Catherine Douglas, *Simple Minders*, ProDesign 27 (Aug.–Sept. 1994).

[19] *Id.* at 28.

The result was a one-page form that can be easily converted to a mailing envelope, together with a set of clear instructions. And the error rate dropped from 66% on the old form to just 10%, saving the Ministry staff "endless time and effort."[20]

13. Australia: Victorian Government — Legal Form[21]

In the mid-1980s, the Law Reform Commission of Victoria (see part 4, highlight 37) produced its monumental four-volume study called *Plain English and the Law*. It should have ended all the debate, then and there.

As a small part of that study, the Commission completely redesigned and rewrote an old legal-style court summons. With the new form, the Victorian government was able to reassign 26 staff members, including 15 from the police force — and save the equivalent of Aus$400,000 a year in staff salaries.

14. Australia: Family Court of Australia — Divorce Forms[22]

In 1994, the Family Court of Australia redesigned its divorce-application forms to meet plain-language guidelines. The Court hoped that the new forms would be easier for appli-

---

[20] *Id.* at 29.

[21] Law Reform Comm'n of Victoria, *Plain English and the Law* 68–69 (1987; repr. 1990); Robert D. Eagleson, *Writing in Plain English* 6, 72–73 (1990; repr. 1994).

[22] Gordon Mills & Mark Duckworth, *The Gains from Clarity: A Research Report on the Effects of Plain-Language Documents* 15–40 (Ctr. for Microeconomic Policy Analysis, Ctr. for Plain Legal Language & Law Foundation of NSW 1996) (available at http://www.clarity-international.net/downloads/Gains%20from%20Clarity.pdf).

cants to use and would reduce the time that its staff spent helping them. The new forms met both goals.

Applicants who filled out the forms on their own, without a legal representative, accurately completed the new ones 67% of the time, compared with 52% on the old ones. For this same group, the number of applications rejected because of errors fell from 42% to 8%. And the new forms reduced the staff's initial processing time by nearly two minutes — from 12.31 to 10.45.

15. U.S.: Cleveland Clinic — Billing Statements[23]

During a symposium sponsored by the Center for Plain Language, Irene Etzkorn, Group Director of Simplification at Siegel+Gale, gave examples highlighting the benefits of plain language, logical structure, and clear design.

One example was a billing statement from the Cleveland Clinic. After it was simplified, the Cleveland Clinic recovered an additional $1 million a month in the months following, thanks to an 80% increase in patient payments. The two versions are online if you'd like to see the difference for yourself.[24]

16. U.S.: Allen-Bradley Company — Computer Manuals[25]

When Allen-Bradley surveyed the marketplace for its programmable computers, it found that the documents that

---

[23] Irene Etzkorn, Workshop Slides, *Amazingly Simple Stuff*, http://centerforplainlanguage.org/events/symposium-2008 (Nov. 7, 2008).

[24] *Id.* at slides 39–41.

[25] Barry Jereb, *Plain English on the Plant Floor*, in *Plain Language: Principles and Practice* 207 (Erwin R. Steinberg ed., Wayne State U. Press 1991).

accompany the product were the second most important factor (after workmanship) in influencing customers to buy. With the help of writing consultants, the company developed a training program for its writers, prepared a style manual for the writers and one for its vendors, and began to review its computer manuals. The new manuals were tested — that critical step again — and further revised before the company put them into the field. And as just one benefit from the new plain-English manuals, calls to the company's phone center fell dramatically — from more than 50 *a day* to only 2 a month.

Below is a short bit from the company's style manual for vendors. Notice the use of personal pronouns and the active voice. People who write for the public should have learned those lessons a long time ago.

Help Users Picture Themselves in the Text

Guideline 1: Address the reader directly.

Original

It is suggested that the wire should be connected to the terminal by the engineer when the switch-box assembly is completed.

Revised

We suggest that you connect the wire to the terminal when you finish assembling the switch-box.

17. U.S.: General Electric Company — Software Manuals[26]

Different company, same story. The technical writers at General Electric Information Services, working as part of individual product teams, develop high-quality manuals for the company's software. In one test, customers who used an earlier version of the manual made about 125 more calls a month than customers who used the clearly written, approved manual. Applying industry standards for the average cost of support calls, the company estimated that it saves from $22,500 to $375,000 a year for each business customer who uses the revised manual.

18. U.S.: Sabre Travel Information Company — Software Booklet[27]

Same story again. A document team at Sabre Travel Information Network developed a short manual to help travel agencies install and use an online guide to the company's computerized flight-information system. The main goal was to reduce calls to the help desk, each of which cost $5.50 (in 1995). The new products — the software and the user manual — did indeed reduce annual calls from 70% of the travel agencies, or 2,100 agencies total, by an average of 210 calls a year for each agency. That's a savings of $2,425,500 (2,100 × 210 × $5.50).

---

[26] Cathy J. Spencer & Diana Kilbourn Yates, *A Good User's Guide Means Fewer Support Calls and Lower Support Costs*, 42 Technical Communication 52 (1995).

[27] C. Al Blackwell, *A Good Installation Guide Increases User Satisfaction and Reduces Support Costs*, 42 Technical Communication 56 (1995).

19. U.S.: Federal Express — Operations Manuals[28]

From 1992 to 1995, a consultant worked with the technical writers at Federal Express to reorganize and revise the company's ground-operations manuals. The team took all the steps: they did a field study of users, tested the old manuals for usability, and compared the manuals to benchmark standards. The team identified the following needs (among others):

- An organization based on user tasks rather than formal job titles.
- A more accessible and readable format.
- Better tables of contents and indexes.
- Improvements in the readability of the text through font changes and writing style.
- Substantially increased use of graphics and tables.

In the testing, readers of the old manuals searched for an average of 5 minutes to find information and found the correct answer only 53% of the time. With the new manuals, the average search time dropped to 3.6 minutes, and the success rate improved to 80%. With some further improvements to the index, the team estimated — very conservatively — that the new manuals would save the company $400,000 in the first year, just in the time that employees spend searching for information. That's not counting costs that flow from getting wrong answers.

---

[28] JoAnn T. Hackos & Julian S. Winstead, *Finding Out What Users Need and Giving It to Them: A Case Study at Federal Express*, 42 Technical Communication 322 (1995).

20. U.S.: Key Bank — Call-Center Manual[29]

In 2001, Key Bank began developing an e-manual, an online reference system for its call-center staff, to replace its old set of procedures. At first, the company had ten employees writing the manual. Then it hired a writing consultant to develop a single format and to train employees in writing for the Web.

After the e-manual was developed, the team timed the call-center staff as it answered calls using the old and new procedures. The staff was able to shave an average of 5.5 seconds off its 22,000 monthly calls — a reduction that the team described as "drastic."[30] The estimated yearly savings were from $64,000 to $72,000. Seconds can add up fast.

21. Canada: Banking Industry — Communications Among Employees[31]

A Toronto-based consulting firm teamed up with a large Canadian bank to systematically study the benefits of shifting to plain language for internal communications. One project evaluated the online documents used by customer representatives who take calls about the bank's products and services. When the documents fail to provide clear information, the customer representatives call a help desk to avoid keeping callers on hold for too long.

The consultants surveyed the representatives; chose five documents to revise, test, and re-revise; and then randomly assigned 30 representatives to two groups: an original-

---

[29] Kathryn Tyler, *Toning Up Communications*, 48 HR Magazine 87 (Mar. 2003).

[30] *Id.*

[31] Rose Grotsky, *Plain Language: Its Effect on Organizational Performance*, 51 Clarity 17 (May 2004); E-mail from Rose Grotsky, Owner of Learning Communications, Inc., to author (Feb. 27, 2010).

document group and a plain-language-document group. These representatives had not seen either the original or the revised documents. When the consultants compared the groups' performance on simple and complex tasks, the plain-language group scored better on all measures at a high level of significance. The results showed that by using plain language, the bank could:

• Improve employee productivity by 36.9%.
• Decrease employee errors by 77.1%.
• Decrease the frequency of calls to the help desk by 17.4%.
• Decrease the duration of calls to the help desk by 10.5%.
• Increase employee satisfaction by 61.2%.

The consultants calculated that, by investing in a full shift to plain language in online documents, the bank could potentially earn a return of Can$3.5 million to $15.2 million over three years. For every $1 spent, the bank could save up to $17.48.

22. U.S.: Homebuyers — Good-Faith Estimates[32]

A good-faith estimate is a disclosure document that gives homebuyers an estimate of loan terms and closing costs; it's one of several disclosures that the Real Estate Settlement

---

[32] Kleimann Communication Group, Inc., *Summary Report: Consumer Testing of the Good Faith Estimate Form*, http://www.huduser.org/publications/pdf/Summary_Report_GFE.pdf (Feb. 8, 2008); U.S. Dep't of Housing & Urban Dev., *RESPA, Regulatory Impact Analysis and Initial Regulatory Flexibility Analysis FR-5180-F-02* 484, http://www.hud.gov/offices/hsg/ramh/res/impactanalysis.pdf; Kleimann Communication Group, Inc., *Gold Quill Work Plan* (unpublished award application).

Procedures Act requires mortgage brokers and lenders to give borrowers.[33]

For many years, the mortgage industry had no clear, uniform good-faith estimate. Thus, borrowers could not easily understand and compare loan terms, like whether they had a variable rate or prepayment penalty or balloon payment. And many didn't understand that actual closing costs could be higher than the estimate.

In 2002, the U.S. Department of Housing and Urban Development began working with a communication consulting firm to develop a new, standardized good-faith estimate. The goal was to provide consumers with readily understandable information and encourage them to shop for the best deal, while not creating a bias against either mortgage brokers or lenders. The consultants conducted seven rounds of testing in three phases. The results show that the new good-faith estimate allows consumers to:

- Identify key loan details.
- Compare across multiple good-faith estimates easily.
- Understand the reciprocal relationship between settlement charges and interest rates.
- Identify the lowest settlement charges in nearly all instances when shown two good-faith estimates.

The study's participants enthusiastically preferred the new estimate to ones they had seen in the past, noting that the language was more understandable and the tables were clear and easy to use. Although every section of the new form applies information-design and plain-language principles, one simple example is the consistent use of white space in the left margin. The space is used only for headings and important callouts. This highlighting of critical information allows borrowers to quickly navigate to important sections.

---

[33] *E.g.*, 24 C.F.R. §§ 3500.7, 3500.8, 3500.15, 3500.21 (2011).

Rules that went into effect January 1, 2010, require mortgage brokers and lenders to give consumers the new good-faith estimate within three days of an application.[34] While the form was being developed, HUD economists estimated that consumers would save nearly $700 per loan on closing costs alone, and that — at about 12.5 million loans a year — annual savings would total over $8 billion.

23. U.S.: General Public — Payday Loans[35]

In 2008, researchers from the University of Chicago Booth School of Business analyzed how the costs of payday loans are disclosed to borrowers. Specifically, the study evaluated how various ways to present information about the costs of payday loans affect people's decisions to continue to borrow from payday lenders.

In 2007, Americans paid an estimated $8 billion in financial charges to borrow more than $50 billion from payday lenders. In a typical payday loan, the annual percentage rate is 443%. While most states mandate APR disclosure on payday-loan transactions, payday lenders typically display their fees in dollars on large pricing menus in their stores (e.g., $15 per $100 of loan). Consequently, people generally mistake 15% for the APR.

The researchers focused on clear disclosure to help borrowers understand the cost — especially long term — of using payday loans. In the study, one group of borrowers received their cash in envelopes with information printed

---

[34] 24 C.F.R. § 3500.7 appendix C (2010). The good-faith estimate is now under the jurisdiction of the Consumer Financial Protection Bureau. *See* http://www.consumerfinance.gov/knowbeforeyouowe.

[35] Marianne Bertrand & Adair Morse, *Information Disclosure, Cognitive Biases and Payday Borrowing*, 66 J. Finance 1865 (2011) (working version available at http://ssrn.com/abstract=1532213).

graphically on the outside. A control group received their cash in plain company envelopes.

Two envelopes with graphics had a substantial effect on borrowers. The first one displayed in a table the accumulated fees (in $) for having a $300 payday loan outstanding for 2 weeks, 1 month, 2 months, or 3 months. It also showed, just for comparison, the fees for borrowing the same amount on a credit card:

How much it will cost in fees or interest if you borrow $300

PAYDAY LENDER (assuming fee is $15 per $100 loan) If you repay in:		CREDIT CARD (assuming a 20% APR) If you repay in:	
2 weeks	$45	2 weeks	$2.50
1 month	$90	1 month	$5
2 months	$180	2 months	$10
3 months	$270	3 months	$15

The second envelope displayed in a chart the typical repayment profile for payday borrowers. The idea was to deflate optimistic expectations about a borrower's ability to repay the loan quickly:

Out of 10 typical people taking out a new payday loan...

| 2½ people will pay it back without renewing | 2 people will renew 1 or 2 times | 1½ people will renew 3 or 4 times | 4 people will renew 5 or more times |

Both envelopes were effective in lowering borrowing amounts. Participants who received the envelopes borrowed about $40 less in their next loan compared to those in the control group — a 17% decline. When applied to the total amount Americans borrowed from payday lenders in 2007, this represents an $8.5 billion decrease.

PLEASING AND PERSUADING READERS

The summaries in this category are organized by the kinds of documents. Thus: legal, 24–38; government, 39–40; internal business, 41–43; medical literacy, 44–47; investment disclosure, 48–49; and technical literature, 50.

In case it would be useful, the following chart organizes all 50 summaries by the kind of documents involved. A couple of summaries show up twice because different reading populations were tested. And a few more might have fit in two different places. There are so many ways to cut and combine all this material.

Document	Summary
Government, for consumers (forms, letters, etc.)	2–3, 5–12, 39–40
Legal, for legal readers (lawsuit papers, opinions)	24–27, 36–38
Legal, for the public (regulations, forms, jury instructions)	1, 13–14, 28–37
Internal business (memos, operating manuals)	4, 19–21, 41–43
Business, for consumers (bills, manuals, buying info)	15–18, 22–23, 48–49

Document	Summary
Medical, for patients	44–47
Technical, for engineers	50

Now back to the evidence on writing to please.

24. U.S.: Judges and Lawyers — Various Legal Passages[36]

In 1987, a colleague and I sent a survey to 300 judges and 500 lawyers in Michigan. We received responses from 425. We asked readers simply to check off their preference for the A or B version of six different paragraphs from various legal documents. One version of each paragraph was in plain language and the other in traditional legal style. Neither the survey itself nor the cover letter referred to "legalese" or "plain English." Rather, the cover letter said the survey was part of an effort to "test language trends in the legal profession." The same study was then repeated in three other states — Florida, Louisiana, and Texas. In Louisiana and Texas, only judges were surveyed. All told, 1,462 judges and lawyers returned the survey. And in all four states, they preferred the plain-language versions by margins running from 80% to 86%.

Here is one of the six paragraphs, taken from jury instructions. (Of course, we didn't always put the plain-language version second.)

---

[36] Joseph Kimble, *Strike Three for Legalese*, in *Lifting the Fog of Legalese: Essays on Plain Language* 3 (Carolina Academic Press 2006).

A [ ]   One test that is helpful in determining whether or not a person was negligent is to ask and answer whether or not, if a person of ordinary prudence had been in the same situation and possessed of the same knowledge, he would have foreseen or anticipated that someone might have been injured by or as a result of his action or inaction. If such a result from certain conduct would be foreseeable by a person of ordinary prudence with like knowledge and in like situation, and if the conduct reasonably could be avoidable, then not to avoid it would be negligence.

B [ ]   To decide whether the defendant was negligent, there is a test you can use. Consider how a reasonably careful person would have acted in the same situation. To find the defendant negligent, you would have to answer "yes" to the following two questions:

   1) Would a reasonably careful person have realized in advance that someone might be injured by the defendant's conduct?

   2) Could a reasonably careful person have avoided behaving as the defendant did?

   If your answer to both of these questions is "yes," then the defendant was negligent. You can use the same test in deciding whether the plaintiff was negligent.

Notice that the B version uses shorter sentences; it addresses jurors as "you"; it avoids redundant pairs like *foreseen or anticipated* and *by or as a result of*; instead of the multiple conditions at the beginning of the last sentence in A (a so-called left-branching sentence), it uses a list at the end of a sentence; and it defines "negligence" positively. Version B is no shorter than version A, but plain language does not always mean the fewest possible words.

25. U.S.: Appellate Judges and Law Clerks — Appellate Briefs[37]

This study involved 10 judges and 33 research attorneys at the California Court of Appeal in Los Angeles. The judges and attorneys were given alternative versions of two paragraphs from appellate documents. One was a headnote, or argumentative heading, taken from an appellate brief. The other was a paragraph from a petition for rehearing. Once again, the paragraphs were not labeled as "traditional legalese" and "plain English." The judges and attorneys were asked to rate the different versions in a number of categories, indicating how persuasive, logical, and comprehensible each version was and whether the writer was from a prestigious law firm.

Can you guess the results? By statistically significant margins, the readers rated the passages in legalese to be "substantively weaker and less persuasive than the plain English versions."[38] What's more, they inferred that the writers of the plain-language versions came from more prestigious law firms.

Here are the alternative paragraphs from the petition for rehearing.

First Version:

PETITION FOR REHEARING

Needless to say, we disagree with much that is set forth in the Court of Appeal's Opinion herein. Nevertheless, this *Petition for Rehearing* is restricted to but a single aspect of the said *Opinion*. This single aspect is the one which pertains to that ratification of an act of his agent which is submitted to flow from the facts as represented by Mr.

---

[37] Robert W. Benson & Joan B. Kessler, *Legalese v. Plain English: An Empirical Study of Persuasion and Credibility in Appellate Brief Writing*, 20 Loyola L.A. L. Rev. 301 (1987).

[38] *Id*. at 301.

Jones to the Superior Court (*Opinion*: page 4, line 2 to page 5, line 2, page 11, line 7 to page 12, line 19). Specifically, we respectfully submit that the Court of Appeal's views relative to the assumed non-existence of such ratification, are predicated upon a factual assumption which is disclosed by the *record* to be *incorrect*. This being so, we submit that the *actual facts*, revealed by the *record*, are such as clearly to entitle us to prevail in respect of the ratification *theory*.

Second Version:

PETITION FOR REHEARING

Although we disagree with much of the Court of Appeal's opinion, we limit this Petition for Rehearing to a single aspect: The question of whether Mr. Jones ratified the act of his agent. The Court found that he did not (*Opinion*, pp. 4–5, 11–12). We respectfully submit that this finding was based upon a misreading of the facts. The Court assumed facts that were clearly contrary to those in the trial record which pointed to ratification. We are, therefore, entitled to a rehearing.

The second version is shorter; it has shorter sentences; it straightens out the tangle of prepositional phrases in the original third sentence ("This single aspect . . . ."); it replaces a lot of inflated diction (*relative to, assumed non-existence, predicated upon, are such as to, in respect of*); it uses verbs (*ratified, assumed*) instead of abstract nouns (*ratification, assumption*); and it's generally straightforward and sincere.

26. U.S.: Lawyers — Judicial Opinions[39]

This survey may have been the first to test judicial opinions. In the mid-1990s, I sent the original and a revised version of a short appellate opinion[40] to a random selection of 700 Michigan lawyers. One was marked O (my own clever code for "original") and the other Y; half the readers saw the O opinion first, the other half the Y opinion.

The revised opinion had an opening summary containing the crucial facts, the deep, or dispositive, legal issue, and the answer; it divided the opinion into short sections with informative headings and began each section with its own summary; it used topic sentences that advanced the analysis; it shortened the average sentence length from 25 words to 19; and it omitted unnecessary cases, other unnecessary detail (beyond the 500 words' worth I had already cut), and unnecessary words. Readers were asked which opinion they liked better, how they rated the two opinions on a 1-to-10 scale, and the top two reasons (from among several provided) why they liked one better than the other.

Out of the 251 lawyers who responded, 153, or 61%, preferred the revised opinion. They rated the (already shortened) original at an average of 6; they rated the revised version at 7. And the 61% that preferred the revised opinion gave as the top two reasons that it left out a lot of unnecessary detail and had a summary at the beginning. Those are two strong lessons for opinion-writers.

The article describing this study reproduces the package that readers received, compares a bunch of examples from the opinions, and even shows the original opinion with the unnecessary detail lined through. Here's the difference just in the all-important opening paragraph:

---

[39] Kimble, *The Straight Skinny on Better Judicial Opinions*, in *Lifting the Fog of Legalese*, *supra* n. 36, at 15–35, 89–104.

[40] *Wills v. State Farm Ins. Co.*, 564 N.W.2d 488 (Mich. App. 1997).

Opinion O:

> Plaintiff Robert Wills filed a declaratory judgment action against defendant State Farm Insurance Company to determine whether defendant has a duty to pay benefits under the uninsured motorist provisions found in plaintiff's policy with defendant. Pursuant to the parties' stipulated statement of facts, the trial court granted summary disposition in plaintiff's favor upon finding coverage where gunshots fired from an unidentified automobile passing plaintiff's vehicle caused plaintiff to drive off the road and suffer injuries. Defendant appeals as of right. We reverse and remand.

Opinion Y:

Summary

> Robert Wills was injured when someone drove by him and fired shots toward his car, causing him to swerve into a tree. He filed a declaratory-judgment action to determine whether State Farm had to pay him uninsured-motorist benefits. The issue is whether there was a "substantial physical nexus" between the unidentified car and Wills's car. The trial court answered yes and granted summary disposition for Wills. We disagree and reverse. We do not find a substantial physical nexus between the two cars because the bullets were not projected by the unidentified car itself.

Note that the revised summary goes beyond the surface issue (was there a duty to pay?) to the deep issue (was there a "substantial physical nexus" — an unfortunate concept — between the cars?). And the revised summary gives an answer as well.

27. U.S.: Judges — Lawsuit Papers[41]

This was the first study to test a complete lawsuit paper — a 3¼-page response to a motion. Studies 26 and 37 tested a complete opinion; studies 32 and 33 tested complete jury instructions; and study 34 tested complete court forms. But even though this more recent study is unique, the results are not.

The author sent 800 surveys to judges across the United States, 200 surveys to each of four different "cohorts": federal trial judges, federal appellate judges, state trial judges, and state appellate judges. Each judge received (1) the original motion and (2) either a plain-English version or what the author called an "informal" plain-English version. As in the other legal studies, the participants were chosen randomly; the cover letter merely said that the sender was conducting a study on legal writing; the versions were not identified as "legalese" or "plain English"; and half the recipients saw the versions in one order, while the other half saw them in the reverse order. A total of 292 judges responded.

The participants were simply asked which version they found more persuasive, along with a request for some demographic information. The published study includes all three versions, but they are too long to reproduce here. The differences between them, though, will sound familiar.

The plain-English version improves on the original version in these ways:

- It's shorter — 2½ pages. So it obviously eliminates unnecessary sentences and words.
- It does away with underlining and all-caps in headings.
- It sets out the four reasons why the court should deny the motion — the critical points — in a vertical list.

---

[41] Sean Flammer, *Persuading Judges: An Empirical Analysis of Writing Style, Persuasion, and the Use of Plain English*, 16 Legal Writing: J. Legal Writing Inst. 183 (2010).

- Its topic sentences provide a better organizational framework.
- Its sentences average 17.8 words, as opposed to 25.2 words.

The informal version of the plain-English sample makes the following additional changes:

- It does away entirely with the formulaic opening ("Plaintiffs, [names], through their attorneys, [names], state as follows in response to . . . .").
- It uses contractions.
- It uses the first person, although just once.
- It's more conversational in tone.
- It further reduces the average sentence length, to 16.3 words.

As in the previous studies, the results were decisive. The author broke them out in various ways, but overall the judges preferred the plain-English version to the original by 66% to 34%. And the demographics made no difference. Preferences were not correlated with state versus federal judge, trial versus appellate judge, rural versus urban area, gender, or years of experience as a judge. The informal plain-English version did not fare quite as well, but 58% still preferred it. The author suggests, based on judges' volunteered comments, that its use of contractions was the main reason for the 8% falloff.

We now have several studies that lead to an inescapable conclusion: legal readers strongly prefer plain language over traditional style. The margins were 61% (summary 26), 66% (summary 27), 67% (summary 37, first study), and from 80% to 86% (summary 24). Solid proof.

28. U.S.: General Public — Various Legal Passages[42]

Now the other shoe drops on legalese. We have a new study — another first of its kind — confirming that the public, too, wants to read plain legal language. Hardly a surprise.

In 2011, the author sent a survey to hundreds of people he targeted by asking law firms to forward the survey to the firms' clients. Then the author asked those people who took the survey to forward it to other friends and contacts. Among other things, readers were asked to choose between 11 pairs of passages. One was written in plain language, and the other included at least one aspect of legalese — passive voice, an abstract noun where a verb should be, an inflated or antiquated word or phrase, or a technical term without an explanation of what it means. Two examples:

(1) I have signed and enclosed the stipulation to dismiss your case.

(2) I am herewith returning the stipulation to dismiss your case; the same being duly executed by me.

(1) Discovery may proceed prior to the judge's consideration of the motion.

(2) Discovery may begin before the judge considers the motion.

Of the 376 responses, 202 were from people who had used an attorney within the previous five years, and the rest were from people who had not. Given the choices, just over 80% preferred the plain-language versions. And the client group preferred it by 5% more than the nonclient group. (Perhaps the clients were still reeling from the effects of traditional style.) On top of that, 41% were "annoyed" by complicated language, and a measly 0.5% were impressed.

---

[42] Christopher R. Trudeau, *The Public Speaks: An Empirical Study of Legal Communication*, 14 Scribes J. Legal Writing __ (forthcoming 2012).

No matter how you slice the results — and the author did it several ways — the vast majority of clients and nonclients want lawyers to mend their linguistic ways.

29. U.S.: General Public — Government Regulations[43]

This study and the next eight tested the comprehensibility of law (a statute or regulation) or other legal documents or language on a nonlegal audience — the public or (in summary 36) the administrators.

In the early 1980s, the Federal Communications Commission reorganized and rewrote its regulations for marine radios on recreational boats. (Apparently, though, the new rules were never incorporated into the Code of Federal Regulations but were put only in a booklet for the public.) The FCC asked the Document Design Center to test the old and new versions. Readers of the old rules got an average of 10.66 questions right out of 20; readers of the new rules got an average of 16.85 right. The average response time improved from 2.97 minutes to 1.62 minutes. Finally, on a scale of 1 (very easy) to 5 (very hard), readers rated the old rules at 4.59 and the new rules at 1.88.

In revising these rules, the FCC adhered to what may be the hardest principle of all to follow because it involves judgment and restraint — don't try to cover every remote possibility under the sun:

> Probably the most important guideline used in revising the FCC's marine radio rules . . . was one that would say "select only the content that the audience needs."

---

[43] Janice C. Redish, *How to Write Regulations and Other Legal Documents in Clear English* 42–43 (1991); Janice C. Redish et al., *Evaluating the Effects of Document Design Principles*, 2 Information Design J. 236 (1981).

The rules for recreational boaters were originally mixed in with rules for ocean liners and merchant ships and were loaded down with exceptions and rules to handle unusual cases.[44]

The cardinal rule of clarity is to put yourself solidly in the minds of your readers: what would they like to know, and how would they like to get it?

30. U.S.: General Public — Statute

In 1995, two colleagues and I revised the South African Human Rights Commission Bill as part of a demonstration project for that country's new Ministry of Justice. I then tested it on 24 staff members at my law school, using 21 multiple-choice questions. Readers of the original version answered 55.6% of the questions correctly; readers of the revised version, 67.5%. The average time to answer all the questions improved modestly, from 39.7 minutes to 36.15 minutes.[45]

31. U.S.: General Public — Jury Instructions[46]

Robert and Veda Charrow conducted one of the first empirical studies of legal language in 1979. They proved that certain pattern jury instructions were hard to understand; they identified problematic grammatical wording and forms; and they showed that correcting the problematic language made the instructions more understandable.

---

[44] Redish et al., *supra* n. 43, at 240.

[45] Joseph Kimble, *Answering the Critics of Plain Language*, 5 Scribes J. Legal Writing 51, 69, 71 (1994–1995).

[46] Robert P. Charrow & Veda R. Charrow, *Making Legal Language Understandable: A Psycholinguistic Study of Jury Instructions*, 79 Columbia L. Rev. 1306 (1979).

To conduct their study, the Charrows presented jury instructions orally — not in writing — to individual participants and then asked them to paraphrase each instruction. Participants accurately paraphrased, on average, only 45% of the most important ideas in each original instruction.

In evaluating the participants' accuracy, the Charrows found that several linguistic and structural elements consistently created problems: nominalizations (nouns formed from verbs), phrases introduced by *as to*, misplaced phrases, missing relative pronouns, legalese, multiple negatives, passive-voice verbs, unnecessary lists, illogical organization, and multiple subordinate clauses in one sentence. The Charrows modified the instructions to reduce or eliminate these difficulties and presented the revised instructions to a second group of participants. They accurately paraphrased an average of 59% of the most important ideas in each revised instruction, a significant improvement.

No doubt 59% is still not good enough, though. We need much more testing of how to improve the instructions themselves and the process of delivering them.[47]

32. U.S.: General Public — Jury Instructions[48]

Two careful studies of jury instructions showed that (1) plain-language instructions are easier to understand than traditional

---

[47] *See, e.g.*, Amy E. Smith & Craig Haney, *Getting to the Point: Attempting to Improve Juror Comprehension of Capital Penalty Phase Instructions*, 35 Law & Human Behavior 339 (2011) (describing two studies of especially difficult legal concepts — aggravating and mitigating factors — in which California's plain-language instructions significantly improved comprehension although it remained low overall, and then the use of "pinpoint" instructions with case-related facts produced greater improvement).

[48] Amiram Elwork, Bruce D. Sales & James J. Alfini, *Making Jury Instructions Understandable* 13–17 (Michie Co. 1982).

instructions, and (2) the type of instruction affects the outcome of a case.

In the first study, mock jurors all watched the same videotaped trial. After the video, they were split into three groups: one received traditional instructions; one, revised instructions; and the other, none at all. Jurors then each filled out a questionnaire about the case facts, their memory and comprehension of the instructions, and their verdict. If the law (properly understood) could not be correctly applied to the juror's stated beliefs about the facts, then the juror's verdict was considered incorrect.

Results: 40% of jurors who received no instructions reached an incorrect verdict, and those who received the traditional instructions improved only to 39%. But only 13% of those with the revised instructions reached an incorrect verdict.

Still, the researchers were concerned that the results might be different if jurors had an opportunity to deliberate, so they conducted a second study. Again, jurors watched a videotaped trial. Afterward, half the jurors received traditional instructions, and the other half received revised instructions. Then they deliberated in small groups to reach a verdict; these deliberations were videotaped. Finally, each participant filled out a questionnaire similar to the one in the first study.

Jurors who received the traditional instructions showed worse comprehension on the questionnaire and during the deliberations. They correctly answered only 58% of the questions on the questionnaire, compared to 71% from jurors who received the revised instructions. This gap was even more pronounced during deliberations: only 25% of the legal assertions and interpretations discussed among jurors with the traditional instructions were correct, compared to 73% among jurors with the other instructions.

Perhaps most concerning of all was the effect that the instructions had on the trial's outcome. Only 46% of jurors who received the traditional instructions correctly applied the law to their own beliefs about the facts of the case. But 70% of the other jurors applied the law correctly.

33. U.S.: General Public — Jury Instructions[49]

The same researchers from the previous summary studied two other sets of jury instructions — one simple and one complex — that were rewritten according to plain-language guidelines. The complex instructions were rewritten twice. Two groups of mock jurors each watched a videotaped trial that corresponded with one or the other set of instructions. In each group, half the jurors received the original instructions and half the plain-language instructions. Afterward, they filled out questionnaires to gauge their comprehension of the instructions.

The plain-language revisions significantly improved comprehension for both the simple and complex instructions. Comprehension of the simple instructions improved from 65% to 80% overall. Comprehension improved even more dramatically for the complex instructions: 51% to 80%.

34. U.S.: General Public — Court Forms[50]

A California study conducted in 2005 tested the use of plain language in two different court forms: a proof of service and a subpoena. Researchers, with the help of the local jury commissioner, selected 60 volunteers and divided them into two equal groups. Group 1 was first tested on the original proof of service and then on the plain-language version of the subpoena. Group 2 was tested on the plain-language proof

---

[49] *Id.* at 43–49.

[50] Maria Mindlin, *Is Plain Language Better? A Comparative Readability Study of Court Forms*, 10 Scribes J. Legal Writing 55 (2005–2006).

of service followed by the original subpoena.[51] For each form, ten questions were read aloud, and participants were given 20 seconds to respond in writing on a blank answer form. The questions were designed to elicit participants' understanding of each form's purpose and the specific steps that each form required.

The scores showed a "marked and statistically significant improvement in reader comprehension" for the plain-language forms.[52] The average score on the plain-language proof of service was 81% accuracy, compared with 61% on the original. The scores on the subpoena showed even greater average improvement: 95% accuracy on the plain-language version and only 65% on the original. Although the researchers did not try to quantify savings, they concluded that more comprehensible forms would have obvious benefits: less time spent explaining the forms and dealing with errors; more confident and self-reliant customers; and reduced printing costs, since plain-language documents are typically shorter (by 40% in the researchers' estimation).

35. U.S.: General Public — Class-Action Notices[53]

A researcher at the University of Georgia, working with the Federal Judicial Center, conducted a study to learn how plain language affected the readers of class-action notices. After selecting 229 stockholders to participate as class members in a fictional securities-fraud class action, the researchers gave half the participants the original version of an actual class-action notice and the other half a plain-language version. The plain-language version used a question-and-answer format,

---

[51] See *id.* at 64–65 for the original and revised proof of service.

[52] *Id.* at 55.

[53] Shannon Renee Wheatman, *The Effects of Plain Language Drafting on Laypersons' Comprehension of Class Action Notices* (unpublished Ph.D. dissertation, U. Georgia 2001).

charts with important dates, less legalese, the active voice, pronouns, shortened sentences, and headings. Participants who received that version performed better in three ways.

First, they spent an average of about 10.2 minutes reading it, compared with 15 minutes for those who received the original version.

Second, when everyone was asked what they would have done with the notice if they had received it at home, those who got the plain-language version said they would be less likely to toss it and much more likely to read it carefully.

	Original Notice	Plain-Language Notice
Throw it away	27%	3%
File it away	12%	3%
Glance at it	59%	37%
Read it carefully	2%	57%

Finally, participants who read the plain-language notice showed greater comprehension, averaging 16 correct answers out of 17, compared with 12 correct for those who read the original notice.

This study, incidentally, shows why plain language figures prominently in so-called nudge theory, which draws on behavioral research for ways to steer people toward making better choices.[54]

---

[54] *See* Cass R. Sunstein, *Empirically Informed Regulation*, 78 U. Chicago L.R. 1349 (2011) (describing many examples of U.S. regulatory initiatives that depend on presenting information in a form that is clear, direct, simple, and salient). Sunstein coauthored the book *Nudge: Improving Decisions About Health, Wealth, and Happiness* (Yale U. Press 2008).

36. U.S.: Law Students and State-Agency Employees — Contract[55]

In the mid-1990s, I rewrote a short services contract that was being used by a Michigan state agency, checked it for accuracy with the agency's director, and tested the two versions on 27 members of the agency staff and 38 law students. Half the readers randomly got one version, half got the other, and they were all asked to answer 14 multiple-choice questions.

For both groups of participants, accuracy and speed improved considerably. The overall percentage of correct answers increased from 53.6 to 78 among the state-agency staff, and from 65.6 to 81 among the law students. The average speed to finish answering improved from 14.8 minutes to 12.4 among the state-agency staff, and from 15.7 to 12.6 among the law students.

Here is one before-and-after provision:

Before:

> 3. The CONSULTANT agrees to fully complete the described assignment and furnish same to the DEPARTMENT by _____ calendar days after notification of Approval, it being fully understood and agreed by the parties hereto that in the event the CONSULTANT shall fail to do so as aforesaid, the DEPARTMENT shall, without the necessity of notice, terminate the services of said CONSULTANT without incurring any liability for payment for services submitted after said due date or shall deduct, as a liquidation of damages, a sum of money equal to one-third of one percent (1/3 of 1%) per calendar day of the total fee if the performance of the entire contract is delayed beyond the due date. Upon written request by the CONSULTANT an extension of time may be granted by the DEPARTMENT in writing, in the event the CONSULTANT has not received from the

---

[55] Kimble, *supra* n. 45, at 69–70, 84.

DEPARTMENT proper information needed to complete the assignment or, in the event other extenuating circumstances occur, the time may be similarly extended. It is further agreed that if a liquidation of damages is imposed pursuant to the aforesaid provisions, any money due and payable to the DEPARTMENT thereby may be retained out of any money earned by the CONSULTANT under the terms of this contract.

After:

5. Due Date for the Work.

The Consultant must complete and deliver the work by ___ calendar days after receiving notice that the Department has approved this contract. The Consultant may ask in writing for more time, and the Department may grant it in writing, if:

(a) the Consultant does not receive from the Department the information needed to complete the work; or

(b) there are other extenuating circumstances.

6. If the Consultant Misses the Due Date.

If the Consultant fails to deliver the work by the due date, the Department may—without having to give notice—choose either one of the following:

(a) terminate the Consultant's services, and not pay for services that are submitted after the due date; or

(b) claim liquidated damages of 1/3 of 1% of the total contract payment for each calendar day late, and subtract this amount from the total payment.

37. South Africa: Lawyers and the General Public — Various Legal Documents[56]

In three different tests on three different groups in South Africa, plain language won out each time — as preferable, more comprehensible, and faster to use.

First, the researchers tested two versions of a judgment (judicial opinion). The study was "inspired" by the study in summary 26[57] and adopted several of the same revisory techniques (reorganized structure, headings, shorter sentences, cutting unnecessary detail), along with some others (numbering paragraphs and using bullets). The two versions, simply marked V and W, were sent with a questionnaire to judges, lawyers, and law students. Of the 382 who responded, 67% preferred the revised version — an even higher number than the 61% in the Michigan study.

Second, the researchers tested on the general public two versions of a divorce action with differences like these:

Before:

> Plaintiff is ordinarily resident within the jurisdiction of this Honourable Court and has been ordinarily resident for a period of one year prior to the issue of summons in this action in the Republic of South Africa and she is domiciled within the said Republic.

After:

> The plaintiff usually lived in the jurisdiction of this Court for one year before she issued a summons in this action.

---

[56] Frans Viljoen & Annelize Nienaber, *Plain Language in South Africa: Report on an Empirical Research Project*, in *Plain Legal Language for a New Democracy* 121 (Viljoen & Nienaber eds., Protea Book House 2001) (together with an unpublished preliminary report).

[57] *Id.* at 122 n. 4.

In all, 144 South Africans participated, and 71.5% preferred the revised versions.

Finally, the researchers asked another group of 60 South Africans to answer a question using different versions of a section from a South African statute. Readers of the plain-language version were far more accurate: 90% answered correctly, compared with 35% for readers of the original version. And they took far less time: an average of 3.9 minutes, compared with 12 minutes for the original.

38. Australia: Lawyers — Legislation[58]

As one of its several demonstration projects, the Law Reform Commission of Victoria redrafted Australia's complex Takeovers Code. They cut it by almost half. They checked the new version for accuracy with substantive experts. And when the Commission tested the two versions on lawyers and law students, those readers comprehended the plain-language version in half to a third of the average time needed to comprehend the original version.

39. U.S.: General Public — Tax Forms[59]

In a project for the Internal Revenue Service, the Document Design Center revised a tax form for the sale of a house. In tests of the old form, only 10% of taxpayers performed well — that is, completed it without significant errors. The Center could not change everything that needed changing because some of the terms appeared in other, related forms. Still, in tests of the revised form, the percentage of taxpayers who performed well increased to 55%. In addition, they

---

[58] Law Reform Comm'n of Victoria, *supra* n. 21, at 69–70.

[59] Anita D. Wright, *The Value of Usability Testing in Document Design*, 30 Clarity 24 (Mar. 1994).

"appeared less confused and less frustrated than those who tested the [old form]. Even without micro-level data, participants' body language suggested that while there were more line items on the revised form, they found it easier to fill out."[60]

40. U.S.: General Public — Ballot Instructions[61]

The National Institute of Standards and Technology conducted a detailed study of 45 volunteer voters in Georgia, Maryland, and Michigan to test the language used in ballot instructions. The voters were given a list of tasks to complete on two different ballots — Ballot A with traditional ballot instructions and Ballot B with plain-language instructions. Half the study group completed Ballot A before Ballot B; the other half completed Ballot B first.

The tables below compare corresponding parts of the instructions.

Ballot A
Press the box of the candidate for whom you desire to vote; yellow will appear in the box. The voter must retouch the selected item to deselect it first in order to change a vote or in case of mistake; then the voter touches the new candidate of choice.
You may choose to vote a straight-party ticket or vote each partisan contest.
Write-In Instructions: Press (Letters) and (Space) as desired. Press (Backspace) to remove mistakes. Press (Accept) or (Cancel) when you are done.

---

[60] *Id.* at 30.

[61] Janice Redish et al., *Report of Findings: Use of Language in Ballot Instructions*, http://www.nist.gov/itl/vote/upload/NISTIR-7556.pdf (May 2009).

Vote for no more than five.

| Accept | / | Reject |

Ballot Summary

Ballot B

To vote for the candidate of your choice, touch that person's name. It will turn yellow.

If you make a mistake or want to change a vote, first touch the yellow box you no longer want. That box will turn gray. Then, touch the choice you do want.

You can vote all at once for all the candidates of one political party for all the races where the candidates belong to a specific party. (This is called a straight-party ticket.)

If you want most candidates from one party but some candidates from another party, you can vote straight party here and change your vote later at a specific race.

To write in a candidate:

- Type the person's first and last names.
- Put a blank space between the first and last name by touching | Space |
- To erase, touch | Backspace |

To complete the write-in, touch | Accept |

If you change your mind, touch | Cancel |

Vote for one, two, three, four, or five.

| For | / | Against |

Review Your Choices

The voting tasks for Ballot A and Ballot B were essentially the same. An example that voters were asked to complete: "Even though you voted for everyone in the Tan Party, for Registrar of Deeds you want Herbert Liddicoat. Vote for him." When the voters got to the Registrar of Deeds contest, they saw that Herbert Liddicoat was not on the ballot. To successfully complete the task, voters had to recognize the need to write him in and do it accurately.

The study measured both the voters' performance and their preference. Overall, voters performed more accurately on the ballot with plain-language instructions than on the traditional ballot, although the difference was just marginally statistically significant. Completing the plain-language ballot first helped voters perform significantly better on the other ballot; the reverse was not true. Researchers also found that education had an inverse relationship with errors made: lower education meant more errors. When asked for their preference between the two ballots, 82% of voters chose the plain-language ballot.

41. U.S.: Naval Officers — Business Memos[62]

Researchers studied the difference between what they called "high-impact" style and "traditional bureaucratic" style. The readers were 262 naval officers (about half of them from the Pentagon), but the document was a general business memo, not one specific to the Navy. As a context, the readers were given a hypothetical case in which a home-office adviser visited a local-office manager. The home-office adviser then followed up with a memo that suggested a way to improve productivity and morale.

---

[62] James Suchan & Robert Colucci, *An Analysis of Communication Efficiency Between High-Impact and Bureaucratic Written Communication*, 2 Management Communication Quarterly 454 (1989).

In the testing, readers of the high-impact memo had a higher percentage of correct answers on each of seven questions. They read the memo in 17% less time (23% less for the D.C. group). And only half as many felt the need to reread it.

Here's how the researchers described the high-impact style:

- The bottom line (the purpose of the report) stated in the first paragraph.
- A contract sentence (stating what major points the report will cover) immediately following the bottom line.
- Short paragraphs, boldface headings that mirror the language in the contract sentence, and lists.
- Simple sentences without a lot of information before or between the main parts (subject–verb–object).
- Subjects and verbs, especially, as close to each other as possible.
- Verbs in the active voice.
- Concrete, easy-to-understand language.
- First- and second-person personal pronouns.

42. U.S.: Army Officers — Business Memos[63]

Another study of "high-impact" style. This time, the researchers wanted to see whether that style is more effective in getting readers to comply with written instructions. They tested 129 Army officers, who were given one of two versions of a memo suggesting that they perform a specific task.

---

[63] Hiluard G. Rogers & F. William Brown, *The Impact of Writing Style on Compliance with Instructions*, 23 J. Technical Writing & Communication 53 (1993).

Readers of the high-impact memo were twice as likely to comply with the memo on the same day they got it.

43. Australia: Insurance Companies — Office Manual[64]

In a study to test the effectiveness of an office manual for an insurance product, 20 staff members who had no experience with the product were split equally into two groups: Group O (old manual) and Group N (new manual, rewritten in plain language). Both groups had ten minutes to complete an exercise using only their manuals for reference. Out of 10 questions, Group O got 3.2 correct while Group N got 6.6.

44. U.S.: General Public — Medical-Consent Forms[65]

Many patients consent to medical procedures without truly understanding the forms they sign. To correct this serious problem, researchers from Carnegie Mellon University developed model consent forms that removed unnecessary information, replaced technical language with more common terms, referred to the patient as "I" or "my," and used simple action words and shorter sentences. The revised forms read at an eleventh-grade (high-school) level, while the original forms read at a nineteenth-grade (doctorate) level.

The example below is from a form consenting to a blood transfusion:

---

[64] Australian Mutual Provident, *Documentation Quality Improvement Team* (1992) (unpublished internal study).

[65] David S. Kaufer et al., *Revising Medical Consent Forms: An Empirical Model and Test*, 11 Law, Medicine & Health Care 155 (1983).

Before:

> It is understood and agreed that the attending physician or his associates or assistants shall be responsible for the performance of their own individual professional acts, and that the blood typing and the selection of compatible blood are the responsibilities of those who actually perform the necessary laboratory tests.

After:

> I understand that in non-emergency situations the lab technicians who perform the blood tests are responsible for determining my blood type. The attending doctor, his associates, or assistants are not responsible for these actions but only for their own actions toward my care.

Researchers tested the blood-transfusion form on a group of 50 college students: half received the original and the other half the revision. Participants each read their form and returned it to the researchers. Researchers then asked everyone the same five questions. Participants who read the revised form answered an average of 4.52 questions correctly; those who read the original averaged only 2.36 correct answers. And participants using the revised form were also faster, averaging 1.64 minutes to answer compared with 2.64 minutes.

45. U.S.: General Public — Medical Pamphlet[66]

In this study, researchers used two versions of a medical pamphlet on polio vaccine. The original pamphlet was from the Centers for Disease Control. The revised pamphlet, which

---

[66] Terry C. Davis et al., *Parent Comprehension of Polio Vaccine Information Pamphlets*, 97 Pediatrics 804 (1996).

was developed by the Louisiana State University Medical Center in Shreveport, simplified the original but still kept the essential information that the doctors believed parents should know. The pamphlets were tested on 522 parents who visited pediatric clinics during July 1993.

The parents' comprehension and reading time improved substantially with the revised version; in fact, reading time dropped from almost 14 minutes to about 4½ minutes. Even more revealing is which pamphlet the parents would be more likely to read. Only 49% said the chances were very good to excellent that they would read the original pamphlet. But 81% said the chances were very good to excellent that they would read the revised pamphlet.

46. U.S.: General Public — Medication Warning Labels[67]

Once more on clear medical information. Researchers from Northwestern University simplified the text and icons used in nine prescription-medication warning labels. The researchers then tested the standard warnings against the simplified warnings with no icons and with the new icons. All three are shown (imperfectly) in these examples:

Standard	Simplified Text	+ Icon

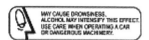   May cause drowsiness. Be careful when driving a car or using machinery.

   Do not drink alcohol.

---

[67] Michael S. Wolf et al., *Improving Prescription Drugs Warnings to Promote Patient Comprehension*, 170 Archives of Internal Medicine 50 (2010).

Standard	Simplified Text	+ Icon
	Limit your time in the sun.	
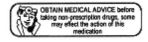	Talk to your doctor before using any over-the-counter drugs.	

A total of 530 patients at medical clinics in Shreveport, Louisiana, and Chicago, Illinois, participated in the study and answered questions about their understanding of each warning. Almost 92% of patients correctly interpreted the simplified warnings with new icons. Similarly, 91% correctly interpreted the simplified warnings without icons. Only 79% correctly interpreted the standard warnings.

47. Canada: General Public — Patient-Information Booklet[68]

In a 2007 study at the University of Alberta, researchers surveyed 65 anesthesiologists to learn some common topics they discuss with their preoperative patients, such as differences between the types of anesthetics and the risks of anesthesia. The researchers developed a patient-information booklet that covered the common topics, explained the anesthesiologist's role, and answered frequent questions about anesthesia. The booklet also contained simple illustrations of hospital settings and relevant procedure. It was written in plain language, at a sixth-grade reading level.

---

[68] Angela Cheung et al., *A Patient Information Booklet About Anesthesiology Improves Preoperative Patient Education*, 54 Canadian J. Anesthesia 355 (May 2007).

Next, the researchers designed a ten-item questionnaire, also written in plain language, to test a patient's ability to understand and retain preoperative information. The researchers divided 322 patients into two groups: Group A did not read the booklet first, answered the questions from common knowledge, and got only 5 out of 10 correct. Group B read the booklet first and got significantly more correct — 9 out of 10.

Both groups contained nearly the same number of non-Canadian patients (educated and not). In group A, the uneducated non-Canadians answered significantly more questions wrong compared with their group's educated Canadians. But in group B, the patients' nationality and education had almost no effect on their number of correct answers.

Plain language improves common understanding even across cultural and educational divides.

48. U.S.: Investors — 10-K Filings[69]

The Securities and Exchange Commission adopted plain-English rules in October 1998 (see part 4, highlight 9).[70] They required public companies to follow plain-English guidelines — short sentences, everyday language, active voice, tabular presentation, no legal jargon, no multiple negatives — when preparing prospectuses. Although the requirement was limited to prospectuses, the SEC encouraged companies to follow plain-English principles in all their documents in an effort to "speak to investors in words they

---

[69] Tim Loughran & Bill McDonald, *Plain English, Readability, and 10-K Filings*, http://www.nd.edu/~tloughra/Plain_English.pdf (Aug. 4, 2009).

[70] 17 C.F.R. § 230.421(b), (d) (2011).

can understand."[71] Many companies took up this charge and made adjustments to additional documents — including 10-K filings, their annual disclosures of company performance.

In 2007, researchers at the University of Notre Dame examined more than 40,000 10-Ks filed from 1994 to 2007 to determine whether they had become more readable since the rule was adopted and to evaluate the effect of any change on investors and companies. The researchers decided not to use traditional readability measures, such as the Fog Index and the Flesch Reading-Ease Score, because their emphasis on the proportion of complex words might overestimate the effect that words such as *corporation*, *company*, *directors*, and *executive* have on the target audience. Instead, the researchers developed their own test — using (among other things) word length, legalese, and personal pronouns — based on the SEC rule. From this more comprehensive test, the researchers concluded that 10-K filings have become increasingly more readable since the rule was adopted. This finding sharply contrasts with a pre-1998 trend toward *less* readable 10-Ks.

As you would expect, making 10-Ks more readable also makes them more useful. The researchers found a positive and significant correlation between improved readability and an increase in the proportion of a company's small trades (1–100 shares) — those typically made by average investors. And increased trading by average investors was a central goal of the rule. Although other factors contributed to an increase in small trades among nearly all investors during that time, the data still showed that "[companies] with greater

---

[71] Quoting Securities & Exchange Comm'n, *A Plain English Handbook: How to Create Clear SEC Disclosure Documents* 4 (Aug. 1998) (foreword by Arthur Levitt) (available at http://www.sec.gov/pdf/handbook.pdf).

improvement in writing style experienced even greater growth in small trades."[72]

Finally, the researchers found that companies that give shareholders greater rights through more democratic policies have significantly more readable 10-Ks.

49. U.S.: Investors — Annual Reports[73]

The Securities and Exchange Commission has noted the particular importance, in annual reports, of the Management's Discussion and Analysis (MD&A) section — a disclosure that gives readers the information necessary to understand a company's financial picture.[74]

A 2007 study tested whether clear, straightforward disclosures make for better informed investors and whether they are more willing to invest when a company's MD&A is written in plain language. Researchers surveyed investors who were active in the securities market but did not have a formal market education. The participants answered questions about readability and investment interest after reading two MD&A samples — one written before a company adopted the SEC's plain-language recommendation and one written after.

A majority of the participants said that the plain-language sample enabled them to make informed decisions and that they would be more willing to invest in the company because the information was easy to understand. So when companies embrace plain-language principles, the likelihood of attracting

---

[72] Loughran & McDonald, *supra* n. 69, at 24.

[73] Shawn B. Harris, *Plain English: The Efficacy of US Securities and Exchange Commission Recommendations in Corporate Annual Reports and Implications for Individual Investors* (unpublished Prof'l Writing & Technical Communication thesis, U. Houston–Downtown 2007).

[74] Securities & Exchange Comm'n, *Interpretation: Commission Guidance Regarding Management's Discussion and Analysis of Financial Condition and Results of Operations*, 17 C.F.R. pts. 211, 231, 241 (2003) (available at http://www.sec.gov/rules/interp/33-8350.htm).

investors increases (as summary 48 confirms). What more incentive do companies need?

50. UK: Institution of Chemical Engineers — Technical Literature[75]

In 1971, a language-and-communication specialist observed that engineers often complained about the dense style of their technical literature but then explained that their bosses and editors wouldn't accept papers written any other way. The engineers said that they felt obligated to write passively and impersonally so that their work would sound impressive. After talking with senior engineers in higher management positions, the specialist was convinced that a small minority was perpetuating the traditional turgid style. So he set out to examine whether engineers, managers, and editors will accept — and might even prefer — direct, active, and personal writing.

In his study, he gave junior and senior members of the Institution of Chemical Engineers six versions of an excerpt from an engineering report, varying only in writing style. Five contained various degrees of technical-writing deficiencies — dense phrasing, passive verbs, scientific jargon, overloaded sentences, long paragraphs. The other one was direct, active, and personal, written in short, plain sentences in three brief paragraphs.

Members were asked to pick the version that was the most comfortable to read, easiest to grasp, and simplest to digest. The direct version was the clear winner: it received more than twice as many votes as the closest dense version — 46% to 18%. And the senior members showed more enthusiasm for the plain-language style than junior members did.

In every field, the lesson is the same.

---

[75] John Kirkman, *What Is Good Style for Engineering Writing?* (Institution of Chemical Engineers 1971).

Coda: A final reminder about the studies in this "Writing to Please" category. They show not only that readers perform significantly better on documents written in plain language but also that readers like them far better than what they're used to seeing — and enduring. This second benefit can only make for readers who are more motivated (dramatically illustrated in summaries 35 and 45), more confident, more trusting, and more satisfied. So it is that plain language could even help to restore faith in public institutions.

Go forth and spread the word.